"We now have many resources that expose the racial divides among women and how they impede our potential. Opie and Livingston offer us something new: how to bridge these divides. With accessible and illustrative examples, they give us a model for our collective liberation. This is hopeful and inspiring work that shows us what can be accomplished when White women choose solidarity with their Black sisters!"

—**ROBIN DiANGELO,** author, *White Fragility* and *Nice Racism*

"If you, like millions of us, desperately wish to find a way to understand each other, bridge our gaps, and work together toward creating a kinder, safer, and more equitable world for everyone—*Shared Sisterhood* is the way forward. It's the first to offer interpersonal and institutional solutions that are novel, engaging, effective, evidence-based, and simultaneously compassionate and challenging. I've observed Opie and Livingston make this happen in real life, in ways that have enriched many lives—my own included—often to the surprise of the most skeptical participants. Opie and Livingston are not only among the most courageous and dignified people I know but are also brilliant, strong, and compassionate."

—**AMY CUDDY,** social psychologist; bestselling author, *Presence*

"A powerful book on how to build bridges across race and gender divides. As leading experts on forming alliances that transcend differences, Opie and Livingston share timely evidence and actionable advice for handling difficult conversations with compassion and vulnerability—and advancing structural and cultural change in your workplace."

—**ADAM GRANT,** #1 *New York Times* bestselling author, *Think Again*; host of TED *WorkLife* podcast

"Grounded in the power of partnership of heart, mind, and soul of women, *Shared Sisterhood* offers a novel approach to collective action for overcoming the diversity challenges organizations face."

—**TSEDAL NEELEY,** Naylor Fitzhugh Professor of Business Administration and Senior Associate Dean for Faculty Development and Research, Harvard Business School; author, *Remote Work Revolution*; coauthor, *The Digital Mindset*

"This book is a blueprint for how women can work together across fraught divides and establish new models of collaboration that have the potential to change the workplace and our lives."

—**MEHRET MANDEFRO,** CEO, Truth Aid Media

"*Shared Sisterhood* is a gift to anyone who cares about building a more equitable and empowering workplace. Opie and Livingston make a deeply compelling case for the importance of authentic connection between employees—and offer a clear, actionable pathway for how we get there as leaders and change makers, one powerful step at a time."

—**FRANCES FREI,** professor, Harvard Business School; author, *Unleashed*

"*Shared Sisterhood* provides a step-by-step guide on how to heal relationships across racial differences, focusing on historically fraught relationships between Black and White women. The book goes further by showing how those healed relationships form the basis of collective action and actual change. This book is a must read."

—**MINDA HARTS,** author, *The Memo, Right Within*, and *You Are More Than Magic*

Shared Sisterhood

Shared Sisterhood

HOW TO TAKE COLLECTIVE ACTION FOR RACIAL AND GENDER EQUITY AT WORK

Dr. Tina Opie
Dr. Beth A. Livingston

HARVARD BUSINESS REVIEW PRESS
BOSTON, MASSACHUSETTS

Library of Congress Cataloging-in-Publication Data

Names: Opie, Tina, author. | Livingston, Beth A., author.
Title: Shared sisterhood : how to take collective action for racial and
    gender equity at work / Tina Opie (PhD) and Beth A. Livingston (PhD).
Description: Boston, Massachusetts : Harvard Business Review Press, [2022] |
    Includes index.
Identifiers: LCCN 2022010868 (print) | LCCN 2022010869 (ebook) |
    ISBN 9781647822835 (hardcover) | ISBN 9781647822842 (epub)
Subjects: LCSH: Women—Social conditions. | Businesswomen. | Solidarity. |
    Equality. | Social justice. | Social responsibility of business.
Classification: LCC HQ1236 .O65 2022 (print) | LCC HQ1236 (ebook) |
    DDC 305.42—dc23/eng/20220520
LC record available at https://lccn.loc.gov/2022010868
LC ebook record available at https://lccn.loc.gov/2022010869

ISBN: 978-1-64782-283-5
eISBN: 978-1-64782-284-2

Dedicated to the people of all races throughout history
who have charted a path toward equity.
May we make you proud.

Contents

Preface

In March 2019, celebrated novelist Kim McLarin asked a poignant question in the *Washington Post*: "Can Black women and White women be true friends?" She writes: "This is what Black women know: When push comes to shove, White women choose race over gender: Every. Single. Time."[1]

This racial divide is not new, nor is it specific to friendship or constrained to relationships between Black and White women only. The continued growth in workforce racioethnic diversity globally makes connections across differences more important than ever before. But, as McLarin notes, if White women—or women from historically power-dominant groups—are more likely to build connections based not on shared gender but on shared racioethnicity, then it makes it difficult for women as a group to advance.[2] It also makes it more difficult for people who are not women to join in the journey toward a more equitable workplace.

Women lead only 6 percent of the top three thousand companies in the United States.[3] For Black women, these numbers are even more stark. There are only three Black women who have ever been *Fortune* 500 CEOs, and only sixteen Black men.[4] In fact, as of 2022, there are only six Black CEOs of *Fortune* 500 companies, two of whom are women (and in total, only forty-one *Fortune* 500 CEOs are currently women of any racioethnic group). Of the forty Asian and twenty Hispanic/Latino *Fortune* 500 CEOs, few, if any, are women.[5] Earnings also reflect gender and racial inequality. Catalyst reported that in 2019 women earned only 81.5 percent of what men earned, and Black, Latinx, Asian, Indigenous, and other women of color experience even greater inequities than White women. For example, in the United States, Black and Latinx women earned 68 percent and 62 percent (of White men's wages), respectively. Internationally, women earned $11,500 in income compared to men's $21,500.

We may forget that such stark statistics represent real people working to have their experiences seen and valued. The push for equity is reflected in social movements that have highlighted and centered viscerally personal and collective experiences, proclaiming the challenges that real people and real groups confront as they navigate racism and sexism in the world. We hear about Black people being murdered in the streets, Asian women being targeted for violence and killed, Hispanic/Latino people being harassed and assumed not to be citizens of the United States, Middle Eastern people being harassed and assumed to be terrorists, Indigenous women who go missing and are never found, disturbing pictures of immigrant children being kept in cages. Social movements from Black Lives Matter, to #MeToo, to Indigenous Peoples' Rights, to Stop AAPI Hate are mounting pressure to act to eliminate such inequitable racist treatment. The societal pressures inspired by these movements have moved into organizations, and multiple business leaders have publicly committed to combat racism and discrimination. Yet, verbal commitments alone are insufficient to dismantle systemic inequities. Smart leaders and companies are now asking themselves, "How can our organization make change?"

To answer this question, we present *Shared Sisterhood*: a philosophy on how to achieve equity across genders and racioethnicity. It is grounded in deep personal introspection and authentic interpersonal connection, with a focus on achieving more equitable outcomes via collective action. Throughout this book, we teach you the practices of *Dig* and *Bridge* to prepare you to authentically connect and engage in collective action toward equity with your Sisters. This *collective action* toward equity in the workplace is when you will work with others—at work or in society at large—to attain your common goal.

This collective action is necessary to achieve equity for women in organizations, particularly those from historically marginalized racioethnic groups, who are still left behind in many ways, even as language promoting diversity and inclusion has become ubiquitous. This book is for women of all racioethnic groups and their colleagues who want to end these inequities, who want real change and demand action rather than mere words. With *Shared Sisterhood*, we focus on what you can do.

To bring you both knowledge and action, we consult our own research and consulting work, secondary academic and historical sources, and an in-depth analysis of our own lives. We use the skills honed during our MBA and PhD degrees in business, the knowledge built during our careers as academics, and the insights gained from our real-life experiences to complement our rich, authentic relationship, bringing *Shared Sisterhood* alive with both the credibility of research and the richness of storytelling and experience.

Black and White Women in the Workplace

McLarin may have asked a specific question about Black and White women for some of the same reasons that we (Beth and Tina) have focused on Black and White women. First, this is our personal

experience; we have moved through this world as a Black woman
and a White woman, and those life experiences animate the workplace examples that we provide. Second, the broken relationship
between Black and White women in the United States is one that
elucidates challenges that may be experienced between members of
other historically marginalized and historically power-dominant
communities. Third, we build from our lived experiences and center
the voices of Black women because it is long past due for those
voices to be heard and valued: the world can learn something from
listening to Black women. We are not saying that the relationship
between Black and White women is the same for women from
Indigenous, Asian, Latina/Hispanic, and Middle Eastern racioethnic
groups in and outside of the United States. What we are saying is that
exploring the challenges between Black women and White women
in the United States and offering solutions to connect the two communities may provide general principles that can also be applied
to strengthen relationships between members of other racioethnic
groups. We hope that women from Indigenous, Asian, Latina/
Hispanic, Middle Eastern, and other racioethnic backgrounds build
upon the Shared Sisterhood foundation that we are establishing. The
key goal of Shared Sisterhood is for *everyone* to be liberated.

We have applied these general principles in a variety of workplace
conversations with women from varying racioethnic backgrounds.
While our backgrounds and specific experiences differed, many of
us were amazed to discover that we could see ourselves in each
other. That coming together to talk about our differences helped us
better understand how to form authentic connections at work with
those outside of our own groups. We invite you to join us as we explore
how the historically tenuous relationship between Black and White
women can help people from various racioethnic backgrounds better

understand how we can all develop more authentic workplace relationships.

A Black Woman's Journey to Shared Sisterhood: Tina Opie

For years, I refused to call myself a "feminist." I bristled at the troubling White supremacist history of feminism in the United States. I rejected the feminist movement for prioritizing gender over racioethnicity and ignoring the unique concerns that I and other Black women confront. To be a feminist, I felt pressure to ignore my Blackness. I was both a Black person and a woman, but my lived experiences taught me that the world would force me to choose. I always chose my Blackness. That meant that throughout my education, I was more likely to be part of the Black student or affinity groups rather than the women's groups.

In graduate school, I participated in a women's student organization. When I attended its meetings, I felt muted. The issues that I wanted to address inevitably concerned the intersection of racioethnicity and gender: yes, women faculty are underrepresented on this campus, but there is only one tenure-track Black faculty member, and that person is a man—and isn't the absence of Black women faculty an issue that this women's organization should champion? My ideas never had a chance to gain traction because they were subordinated to a focus on broader (read: White) issues of gender. When I joined the Black Student Union, I felt more at home around other Black people who understood critical elements of my identity, jokes, and upbringing than I did around White women, who often seemed foreign to me. We seemed separated by a chasm of racism and stereotypes.

Preface

Once I graduated and joined the workforce, I observed this same racial chasm between women in my workplace. Why, if feminism implies and inspires such strong connection, haven't Black and White women been able to connect and collectively address workplace gender inequity? My personal workplace challenges with racism and sexism immediately came to mind as I thought about this problem. Members of historically marginalized groups are often asked to shrink themselves, to conform to dominant notions of femininity and professionalism. I wanted to create a solution to this problem that enlarged rather than shrank, that connected rather than divided. Perhaps ironically, I recognized that fully examining our racioethnic divisions was an important step to overcoming them.

Inspired by the bold admonishments of the late bell hooks to consider the interlocking natures of our common experiences as women, I knew I needed to create a bold framework that rejected the patriarchal White supremacist professionalism that prioritized the transactional nature of business over authentic connection and liberation.[6] I asked: How can we use our similarities and our differences as women to help all of us be liberated? Shared Sisterhood enlarges feminism to create a space where no one is "the other."[7] The beauty of Shared Sisterhood is that it centers the experiences of historically marginalized groups, and it necessitates the involvement of people from historically dominant racioethnic groups so that we can actually dismantle systems of inequity. Using the foundations of power and history, Shared Sisterhood requires everyone to dig into their preconceptions and bridge across their differences, working through the discomfort and the difficulty together so that we can collectively act.

Ideas swirled in my head as I pondered how best to frame this construct that melded history and business, gender and racioethnicity, process and outcome, finally shelving it as I reflected further. Years passed, and occasionally I would pull out the draft to review it. There was something there, but I didn't quite know how to bring it to fruition. Fortunately, in January 2018, it became clear that I needed a White Sister to help me: a paradigm exhorting sisterhood needed a sisterhood to create it. I sought to find a partner to see what we could create together. The authentic relationship between Beth and me became the meta-foundation for Shared Sisterhood, as the seed that was planted years ago was watered and grown together.

A White Woman's Journey to Shared Sisterhood: Beth Livingston

When Tina first spoke to me about her concept of Shared Sisterhood, it was in response to a larger conversation she and I were having in the wake of the growing #MeToo movement. She sent me an email and brought up "a shelved paper I have on Shared Sisterhood that explores why Black and White women haven't made larger collective bounds in the workplace." She had me at this sentence. Our work since that moment has exemplified the very concept that we write about in this book; we built our authentic connection to bridge across our differences to act together.

My childhood led me to understand the importance of building relationships across racioethnic lines from an interpersonal perspective, though it took a number of years for me to truly understand the systemic issues that existed all around me as a young White child growing up in Kentucky. My brothers were a decade older than I am and our house was always filled with teenagers when I was a young girl. This meant that I grew up with a network of "older brothers" who were predominantly Black teenagers. They laughed with me, read me stories, played games with me, and teased me as if I was their own sister. These individual connections, however, did not automatically make me "Shared Sisterhood" material as I grew into adulthood. As I got older, I learned how much more work I needed to do to understand my "brothers" and how their experiences in life differed from my own. I learned that racism was not just an individual challenge that one person's love could overcome; it required a consistent effort to dig into how my own preconceptions may perpetuate inequity in ways I didn't intend.

I became very focused on racial and gender equity when I was in college at the University of Kentucky. Although my childhood surrounded me with racial diversity in my personal life, I did not quite understand the history of power and prejudice in society or at work and I devoured books on the topic. It was in the early days of the internet, and few places existed online to talk about these issues—so I relied on seminars and book discussions and my own understanding. This insatiable desire to understand—and to fix—the inequity I had learned about was grounded in my personal experiences and love for the men and women I grew up with, and it led me to a career in academia, where I started to research the causes of the gender wage gap and gender/racial prejudice and bias. I learned a lot from this research—but I still couldn't figure out how to reassure the people in my studies, my MBA students, and the employees I met when I worked with companies that I had solutions for their struggles with racism and sexism at work. I built relationships with men and women whose racioethnicities were different from my own, but could this difference actually play a role in reducing workplace inequity? These relationships helped sustain me throughout my life, but could they provide a solution? To be honest, I did not even know where to start. I knew I cared, I knew I was frustrated—but what could I do?

So, when I received that email from Tina, and we began to work on bringing Shared Sisterhood to the world, all the pieces began to fit together. My childhood, the books I had read, and my relationships could all be part of a solution that would prioritize and center authentic relationships, while not ignoring the work that goes into building and sustaining them. Instead of seeking the solutions that others would create, we could step up and present our own.

Working Together

We know that Shared Sisterhood is a powerful tool. How? Because the book that you are holding in your hands is the result of Shared Sisterhood between the two of us, Beth and Tina. This book could not have been written by either one of us individually. To write it, we needed to bring our gender and our different racioethnicities together. Our individual perspectives were insufficient to create a model like Shared Sisterhood.

As soon as we decided to work together, Shared Sisterhood sparks flew. We published an article in *Harvard Business Review* (HBR) in 2018 based on a survey of HBR readers about their workplace experiences of inclusion. This article piqued the interest of the *HBR Women at Work* podcast, where we summarized our findings on inclusion, following up with another article on HBR.org in 2019 (reprinted in fall 2020). We published an academic article in *Organizational Dynamics* soon after. We also made media appearances as audience members became increasingly curious about how Shared Sisterhood could help their organizations become more diverse, inclusive, and equitable.

All the while we thought, "How do we bring Shared Sisterhood to people who can use it?" Then, George Floyd, Breonna Taylor, and Ahmaud Arbery were all murdered over the course of a few months in 2020. Tina's phone began to ring off the hook as she saw a proliferation of consulting clients who were struggling with how best to address the collective pain that many employees were experiencing. Shared Sisterhood seemed to be a helpful framework. As professors of business, we found that companies were anxious to know what to do, what to say. We were encouraged to see some White people fervently protesting alongside Black people and people from all racioethnic categories in the streets, online, and in the workplace. But a critical question was: What comes next?

We needed to meet the moment. Tina recorded a heartfelt plea to the White women in her life and reinvigorated an online community that has grown to greater than four thousand members. Beth and Tina hosted weekly online and videoconference check-ins with members, spoke to podcasts and radio and television programs, and wrote about our thoughts. But still: What more could we do? This book is us meeting a moment—a moment that still exists today—that required bold action grounded in a new approach to diversity, equity, and inclusion.

About the Book

With *Shared Sisterhood*, we seek to create a different reality. The current status quo in organizations is characterized by "masculinized" power structures, such that people reward and elevate behaviors that are typically characterized as masculine in nature. Dominance, succeeding at the expense of others, and even aggression are seen as leadership-worthy attributes.

Shared Sisterhood is different. It is a philosophy that embraces authentic connection and collective action, not a transactional, every-person-for-themselves approach. Although we reject an "individual only" solution, we do not reject the role of individuals in a solution. We argue that individuals may be the only ones who can challenge historical institutional structures (including corporations), but *only* when those individuals act to address institutional-level systems while working with others. Shared Sisterhood helps you to reflect on yourself as an individual, develop authentic interpersonal connections, and then use those relationships to collectively dismantle systemic inequities using the tools of Dig and Bridge. Dig is a tool for thinking deeply about your own preconceptions about racioethnicity and gender. Bridge is a tool for forging authentic connections with people across differences. And together, these tools will help you to form the foundation for collective action. For women of different racioethnic backgrounds and their colleagues in organizations for whom this is a critical goal, we provide stories and research to make you think, deep questions to consider, and actions to pursue.

Shared Sisterhood is not just an outcome. It is a way of thinking. In this book, we do not prioritize comfort, we prioritize change, and we welcome you to begin your journey in Shared Sisterhood—we are still on ours every day. Always bridging, always digging, and always working toward collective action, together.

Frequently Asked Questions

Connecting authentically via Shared Sisterhood requires clear communication. In that spirit, let us lay out some Frequently Asked Questions about our terminology, so we are all on same page before we begin:

1. What are racioethnicity and racism, and why do they matter?

Throughout this book, we use the term *racioethnicity* to encompass the broader variation in physical and sociocultural differences that have meaning across cultures.[8] Historically marginalized racioethnic groups in the United States include people identifying as Black/African American, Hispanic or Latinx, Asian or Pacific Islander, and Native/Indigenous (among others). There are debates about how to define racism in academia that include individual and systematic components.[9] For our purposes, we define racism as power+prejudice.[10] Prejudice refers to preconceived notions about a person or group, not based in reason or actual experience, and it is related to interpersonal bias. But when you add systemic power to that equation—or the ability granted by societal position, history, or other factors to exert force over someone—it becomes racism. This follows sociological work on racism and textbooks on teaching diversity and social justice, and it is echoed by contemporary theorists like Robin DiAngelo and Ijeoma Oluo.[11] In this way, while any group can express prejudice or bias, or enact discriminatory behaviors based on those biases, racism is enacted by a dominant group that has power in that context (such as the power that White people have as the most powerful racioethnic group in the United States). For example, an individual from a historically marginalized group might believe that White people are unkind (racial prejudice) or choose not to associate with a White individual (racial discrimination). However, given existing power dynamics in the United States, the individual from the historically marginalized group, regardless of those opinions, would not be able to create power structures at the collective level to subject members of the dominant group to their opinions.

2. How will these power dynamics affect the process of Shared Sisterhood?

Because of the difference in power dynamics in the United States and around the world, people from historically marginalized racio-ethnic groups and those from historically dominant groups will likely enter their Shared Sisterhood journeys at different places. The Dig component of Shared Sisterhood is designed with these differing entry points in mind. Specifically, the Dig process helps us uncover and address the deep-seated issues and roadblocks that dominant group members may have due to racist ideologies and systems; it also helps us redress the racialized trauma that histori-cally marginalized group members may experience as a result of racism. Acknowledging and understanding the existing racioeth-nic power structure allows us to meet people where they are, so that we can all grow together.

3. Why do you focus on White and Black relations in the United States?

Both of us were born and raised in the United States and have been participants in the US culture since our birth. Although Shared Sisterhood as a philosophy and worldview, and the pro-cess we present in this book for achieving it, will apply to contexts outside of the United States, our framing is based on the US con-text due to our own experiences as a Black and a White woman in this country. This framing allows us to talk about our own experi-ences and to delve deeply into the literature on racial prejudice and racism that exists in the US context. That's not to say we're ignoring other historically marginalized people in this process. It is important to note that the experiences of Black and White women are not necessarily the same as those of women from Indigenous, Asian, Latinx/Hispanic, or Middle Eastern racioethnic groups, whether inside or outside the United States. But the challenges that exist for Black women and White women in the United States, and the solutions we offer that are grounded in this context, can illustrate general principles and processes that can strengthen relationships between members of other racioethnic groups as well.

Shared
Sisterhood

1

Shared Sisterhood to Dismantle Inequities

On the morning of March 3, 1913, Ida B. Wells-Barnett prepared for the Illinois delegation's march in the 1913 suffrage parade in Washington, DC. The parade was strategically scheduled for the day before President-elect Woodrow Wilson's inauguration to ensure large crowds. According to *Ms.* magazine, more than five thousand costumed parade participants, who hailed from all forty-eight states plus other countries, were surrounded by floats, bands, golden chariots, and squads on horseback.[1] The festive occasion was designed to gain "Votes for Women." The marchers soon encountered an angry crowd that, by some estimates, had ballooned to over five hundred thousand. The marchers were attacked by the crowd and, according to White House archives, over one hundred women were hospitalized while the police did little to assist the marchers.[2]

Wells-Barnett was all too familiar with such violence. Twenty-one years earlier, on May 7, 1892, Wells-Barnett's Memphis newspaper office, home of the *Free Speech and Headlight*, was destroyed by a White mob angered by Wells-Barnett's writings on lynchings. The lynching mob threatened Wells-Barnett with bodily harm, and she eventually relocated to Illinois.[3]

With such visceral personal experiences, Wells-Barnett's anticipation of the parade was likely colored by her own experiences with angry White mobs. Unfortunately, the White women parade organizers also prioritized other White women over their sisters of other racioethnicities, embracing anti-Black racism. For example, the president of the National Women's Suffrage Association, Anna Shaw, was known to be hostile to Black women and demanded that Black women march in the all-Black delegation at the back of the parade rather than with their state delegations. Shaw was on the record as proclaiming: "You have put the ballot in the hands of your black men, thus making them political superiors of white women. Never before in the history of the world have men made former slaves the political masters of their former mistresses!"[4]

Despite the broader anti-Black context, even within the women's suffrage movement, Wells-Barnett was determined to walk in the parade, and not with the all-Black delegation in the back.

According to the *Chicago Tribune*, Wells-Barnett asserted her choice to march with the full Illinois delegation, particularly addressing two White women, Grace Trout and Clara Barck Welles, who were leaders of the Illinois delegation to the parade. Trout stated that if it were up to her, she'd allow Wells-Barnett to march. But as the national association had "decided it is unwise," she would abide by its decision.

At that point, however, Virginia "Joan of Arc" Brooks (a White woman) intervened and said, "It would be autocratic to exclude men or women of any color. . . . We should stand by our principles. If we do not, the parade will be a farce." Belle Squire (another White supporter) concurred. Rather than allowing racist social norms to distance her from Wells-Barnett, Brooks recognized the common humanity that she shared with Wells-Barnett in her speech, regardless of racioethnicity. It was a risk for them to speak up in support of Wells-Barnett and challenge the norms of racial inequity that characterized the women's movement, but they did it anyway.

Trout, facing pressure from other White members of the parade who had threatened not to march if Black women were allowed to march alongside them, refused to allow Wells-Barnett to march with the delegation. Brooks and Squire offered to walk with Wells-Barnett in the Black delegation in solidarity, but Wells-Barnett left the room.

As they prepared to march, Brooks and Squire looked for Wells-Barnett but could not find her, and, though fearful that she had left out of disgust, they soon began to march. But as the Illinois delegation approached Pennsylvania Avenue, Wells-Barnett suddenly emerged from the crowd on the sidewalk and confidently assumed her place between Brooks and Squire. Flanked by her two White women Sisters, Wells-Barnett finished the parade with the Illinois delegation, as she had planned (figure 1-1). Brooks and Squire's risk-taking engendered trust with Wells-Barnett and continued a strong partnership that had roots in Wells-Barnett's founding of the Alpha Suffrage Club in 1911 with their help.

This example of White and Black women working together demonstrates the power of Shared Sisterhood in three key ways that we will draw upon throughout the rest of the book:

FIGURE 1-1

Ida B. Wells-Barnett marching with other suffragists in a parade in Washington, DC, 1913

Source: Chicago Daily Tribune, March 5, 1913, page 5.

1. There was a clear divide between the women involved in the 1913 parade, a divide that needed to be bridged. On one hand, the organizers felt that they should adhere to racist social strictures that dictated that Wells-Barnett would have to walk with the all-Black delegation at the back of the parade. On the other hand, Wells-Barnett, Brooks, and Squire engaged in

Shared Sisterhood as they attempted to eliminate racial inequities in their quest for voting rights for all women.

2. Despite their stated best intentions, the White women leaders of the Illinois delegation failed to take a risk and stand up for their espoused beliefs. Their actions conveyed a lack of Shared Sisterhood and harmed the very people they claimed they wanted to help. Empathy alone was not enough; positive impact via authentic connection can be assessed by whether or not participants *actually* reduce racioethnic inequities. The distinction between one's intent and one's impact is critical to Shared Sisterhood.

3. The racial dynamics of the 1913 parade parallel contemporary events. The presence—or lack—of Shared Sisterhood has continued into the current era of women's activism. For example, the Women's March, held in January 2017, was attended by an estimated three million people in the United States, with over two hundred thousand protesters in Washington, DC, alone, making it the largest protest in the District since the Vietnam War. Yet, despite its broad appeal, the march was criticized for its narrow focus and lack of attention paid to the intersectional concerns of women in the United States. In particular, critics balked at the primary attention given to White women's perspectives about issues confronting women. Intersectional analysis will facilitate more nuanced solutions to issues confronting women by focusing on authentic connections across differences, grounded in personal introspection. Shared Sisterhood is such an approach.

This schism between Black and White women in the United States was evident in the experiences of Ida B. Wells-Barnett a century ago.

Given the laws and social norms prohibiting interracial relationships at that time, it is not difficult to believe that Wells-Barnett and Squire must have developed a relationship characterized by empathy, trust, vulnerability, and risk-taking as they fought for equal rights in the face of racism. These same characteristics can help today's employees—people of all racioethnicities—to develop relationships that benefit these employees and the organizations that employ them. Regrettably, the divide between White and Black women at work can still be seen, anecdotally and in research.[5] Given that we are a Black woman and a White woman from the United States, this specific historical context will permeate much of what we discuss in this book. Yet, Shared Sisterhood is designed to foster authentic connection across various racioethnicities and other identity differences (such as religion, age, and so forth).

The 1913 march is an excellent demonstration of when Shared Sisterhood is needed to bridge a divide, where it can go wrong despite good intentions, and how true collective action for equity requires a focus on how different women experience issues of inequity. Building partner-based coalitions grounded in trust, empathy, vulnerability, and risk-taking can lead to authentic emotional connections and interactions that endure and build, promoting collective action for women in organizations.

The Need for Shared Sisterhood Today

History provides examples of Shared Sisterhood in action (or inaction) and also illustrates the ways in which women as a group have been denied positions of leadership. The statistics we introduced in the preface on gender and racial inequality are indisputably stark for women—particularly those from marginalized racioethnic groups, and they reflect cultural norms about gender and racioethnicity that Shared Sisterhood seeks to address.

The primacy of masculine-coded strategies and leadership in business and management is well established. Research conducted by the *Wall Street Journal* in 2020 demonstrated the poor job that organizational leaders were doing when it comes to promoting women to the upper echelons of organizations.[6] In the article, Mike Wirth, CEO of Chevron, stated that Chevron's leadership model focused on someone "aggressive, take-charge, has all the answers," resulting in women high-potentials being overlooked. It took an external firm to broaden the metrics for Chevron leadership to include less masculine-typed attributes, such as accountability and building consensus. In too many companies, it's still "think leadership, think male." People who are masculine and assertive are seen as leaders, and these traits are also more likely to be associated with men than women, and these effects also vary by racioethnicity of the woman in question.[7] But we often see the conversations around rectifying these disparities couched in the same masculine language around competition and aggression where, for instance, White women feel that gender should trump racioethnicity in the competition for equality.[8] Many approaches to equity echo these zero-sum approaches that are grounded in masculine norms of competition and aggression.

Shared Sisterhood is different. Communion and warmth have long been linked to notions of the feminine. Norms of connection, empathy, care, and humility are seen as stereotypically female, and in fact men who engage in these behaviors are ostracized, while women who do so are not seen as leadership material.[9] We argue that such behaviors not only characterize good leadership, but that they can serve as the foundation for authentic emotional interactions at work, creating a latticework upon which true collective action can be grown.

Shared Sisterhood is the antidote to male-typed organizational advancement that privileges individual competitiveness. Importantly, Shared Sisterhood requires women to work together across their racial differences to create it. Unfortunately, current research suggests that the contemporary workplace is ripe for continued mistrust between women of different racioethnicities. For instance, a McKinsey study found that, compared to other women, Black women experience more workplace microaggressions. And Angelica Leigh and Shimul Melwani have demonstrated how large societal traumas related to racioethnicity—like the targeting of Asian Americans or shootings of Black men by police—can spill over to make people avoid their coworkers who are of different racioethnicities than theirs.[10] Because White women have often made strides toward equity at a faster pace than their women colleagues of color (for instance, Black women comprise less than 4 percent of management positions compared to about 30 percent for White women), there may be residual and continuing mistrust that exists between them. We argue that Shared Sisterhood is particularly helpful to repairing mistrust that may exist between White women and women of color in the United States and beyond.

What Is Shared Sisterhood?

For years—in all honesty, for decades—I (Tina) repeatedly failed to connect with White people about workplace racism. Conversations with White colleagues about workplace racism often led to defensiveness, emotional distancing, and worst of all, few if any substantive changes in workplace diversity, equity, or inclusion.

One day, I asked myself, "Tina, what in the world is going on? These are decent people. Why is it so difficult to talk about and change basic things like the fact that the employee base is shockingly lacking in racioethnic diversity and the fact that salary disparities exist between racioethnic groups?"

Shared Sisterhood is a philosophy that emphasizes collective action toward dismantling racial and gender inequity at work, grounded in deep introspection and authentic emotional connections. These authentic connections are characterized by four components: empathy, vulnerability, trust, and risk-taking. These four components are not arbitrary. Together, they address how individuals experience relational processes: In this relationship, what beliefs, emotions, and actions do I and my relational partner(s) experience? Table 1-1 outlines key questions addressed by each of the four components. We then provide a detailed discussion of each component in turn, demonstrating how they come together to create the authentic emotional connections Shared Sisterhood encourages.

TABLE 1-1

The four components of authentic connection

	Belief/emotion	Action
Me	**Trust:** Do I believe that they have my best interests at heart?	**Vulnerability:** Am I willing to put myself at risk for them?
Them	**Empathy:** Can I understand or relate to their feelings and perspectives?	**Risk-taking:** Are they willing to put themselves on the line for me?

Source: Reprinted from *Organizational Dynamics: Special Issue on Power and Politics*, Tina Opie and Beth Livingston, "Shared Sisterhood: Harnessing Collective Power to Generate More Inclusive and Equitable Organizations," Copyright 2021, with permission from Elsevier.

Empathy

A classic case of empathy-building is demonstrated in the work of Jane Elliott and her famous "blue-eyed/brown-eyed" exercise from the 1960s. Elliott was a teacher in an almost entirely White school district in Iowa, and the day after Martin Luther King Jr. was assassinated, a little boy came to her with a question. He asked: "Why'd they shoot that King?" He had very little context for the story that was dominating the news, and his question demonstrated to Elliott that there was an empathy gap that she felt compelled to fill.

Elliott was not a researcher, but she was an innovative teacher. And she knew that she needed to find a way to help her schoolchildren understand what it was like to feel what others were feeling and see the world from their perspective. Her class of all-White children had few experiences associating with Black children and even fewer opportunities to understand what it was like to grow up as a member of a historically marginalized group in the United States. She vowed to teach her third grade class about empathy with Black Americans via an exercise using eye color as analogous to skin color. And the "blue-eyed/brown-eyed" experiment was born.

As shown in the *Frontline* PBS special on her work, when her class returned to school the next day, the blue-eyed children were told they were smarter, nicer, neater, and better than the children with brown eyes. She reversed these roles on the second day, telling the brown-eyed children that they were actually in the dominant group. The children began to treat each other poorly, based only on the color of their eyes. The students who were told that they were not as good performed more poorly in class and suffered from low self-esteem—and those who were told they were better lived up to those expectations as well. When she finally debriefed the exercise with them, they had learned a valuable lesson in empathy. As Elliott said, "They found out how to hurt one another and they found out how it feels to be hurt in that way and they refuse to hurt one another in that way again."[11]

Collective action is unlikely to occur without empathy. Empathy is a critical component of Shared Sisterhood because it is one of the most fundamental building blocks of social connection.[12] During large social movements toward racial justice in the United States, empathy inspired social media posts such as "Imagine if it were your kid." Empathy was the impetus for Barack Obama's speech in reaction to the Trayvon Martin case, where he said, "This could have been my son."[13] The premise is that, to build empathy, you try to see the world from someone else's point of view and understand their feelings. And when it comes to building connections across racio-ethnicity, that means empathizing with those who look different from you.

There is a long history of research in social psychology on empathy and perspective-taking, which is described as the "cognitive ability to understand the viewpoint of others and share their feelings."[14] Empathy and perspective-taking go hand in hand in the study of how people relate to one another, with work on restorative justice focusing on empathy as the "emotional root of solidarity" and perspective-taking as a process to induce empathy in which people put themselves in the shoes of other people.[15] Active perspective-taking is when a person tries to understand the thoughts, motives, and/or feelings of a target, and why they think or feel that way.[16] The ability to feel what others feel (empathy) and see the world as others see it (perspective-taking) are often inextricably linked, in both research and practice. Thus, when we talk about empathy, we are referring to both of these abilities together.[17]

Vulnerability

The second component of Shared Sisterhood is vulnerability. Making oneself vulnerable can be a big ask. As the author Brené Brown says, "Vulnerability is about having the courage to show up and be seen" as your whole self. Brown continues her discussion of the importance of vulnerability when she says, "Yes, we are totally exposed when we are vulnerable. Yes, we are in the torture chamber that we call uncertainty. And, yes, we're taking a huge emotional risk when we allow ourselves to be vulnerable. But there's no equation where taking risks, braving uncertainty, and opening ourselves up to emotional exposure equals weakness."[18] Making ourselves vulnerable as we interrogate our deepest beliefs about racism is a sign of courage because it requires personal risk.

If you admit to yourself and others that you have struggled with prejudice, or engaged in racist thoughts or actions, it means risking your reputation and friendships. To understand your own perceptions and biases about racioethnicity, you have to be willing to make yourself vulnerable to self-judgment (when confronted with deeply held beliefs that might conflict with your self-image), criticism from others, and the shame that may accompany such criticism. Instead of choosing defensive reactions to this criticism, Sisters are encouraged to choose reparative reactions that emphasize their willingness to listen and change. Research has demonstrated that incidents of moral failure can lead to feelings of shame, and that this shame can either result in pro-social, or positive actions toward repairing trust, or defensive, anti-social actions to avoid condemnation. When someone perceives that their overall self-image is threatened by their mistakes, they are more likely to avoid or conceal their mistakes, behavior that is the antithesis of demonstrating vulnerability on the path to growth.[19] But perceiving such mistakes as moral lapses associated with personal failings that can be righted may be more likely to lead to growth that benefits society.[20] Making yourself vulnerable in moments of failure or lapses in judgment is difficult. But it is this vulnerability that distinguishes surface-level attempts at empathy and connection from those that produce more lasting change.

When someone tells you something about themselves that puts themselves at risk—personally, psychologically, or politically—it makes them vulnerable. But it can also demonstrate their humanity, with personal storytelling of one's own journey being a valuable tool for demonstrating the authenticity of your connection and facilitating trust.[21]

Trust

Interpersonal trust is a critical construct in management and social psychology. Building trust between two people can involve multiple components.[22] The components of trust between two people at work can include integrity (honesty), competence (skills to do the job), consistency (reliability), loyalty (benevolent motives), and openness (willingness to share ideas freely).[23] No matter whether the relationships are between employees and bosses or between coworkers, integrity and competence seem to be the most important components for perceiving trustworthiness, in that people building relationships grounded in trust are looking for honesty and truthfulness, and someone they can trust to do their job well.[24] Building this trust is important. It increases motivation for team performance, and it can even reduce stress.[25] It's no wonder that learning to trust others, and making yourself more trustworthy, is a critical component of authentic connections in Shared Sisterhood.

There are various ways to think about trust and how it develops—or disintegrates. When a relationship is characterized by high trust, people have hope and faith in one another, and confidence in their intentions and actions.[26] But distrust and trust can exist simultaneously in a "trust but verify" type of way. To establish authentic connections, you have to increase the presence of trust while decreasing distrust—moving from the assumption of harmful motives and defensive postures to the sharing of values and opportunities.[27] Figure 1-2 demonstrates that trust and distrust are separate but related things. And both

FIGURE 1-2

Integrating trust and distrust: alternative social realities

	2	**4**
High trust, characterized by hope, faith, confidence, assurance, initiative	High-value congruence Interdependence promoted Opportunities pursued New initiatives	Trust but verify Relationships highly segmented and bounded Opportunities pursued and downside risks/vulnerabilities continually monitored
	1	**3**
Low trust, characterized by no hope, no faith, no confidence, passivity, hesitance	Casual acquaintances Limited interdependence Bounded, "arms-length" transactions Professional courtesy	Undesirable eventualities expected and feared Harmful motives assumed Interdependence managed Preemption: best offense is a good defense Paranoia
	Low distrust, characterized by no fear, absence of skepticism, absence of cynicism, low monitoring, nonvigilance	**High distrust, characterized by fear, skepticism, cynicism, wariness and watchfulness, vigilance**

Source: Adapted from R. J. Lewicki, E. C. Tomlinson, and N. Gillespie, "Models of Interpersonal Trust Development: Theoretical Approaches, Empirical Evidence, and Future Directions," *Journal of Management* 32, no. 6, figure 1, p. 1003, copyright © 2006 by the Journal of Management. Reprinted by Permission of SAGE Publications, Inc.

are critical for Shared Sisterhood. As we will argue in subsequent chapters, members of specific groups with specific social histories and experiences may have different needs—they may find themselves in different boxes, at different times, with different people.

Trust can develop in different ways within a relationship or context. It happens over time, yes, but it also develops in fits and starts, nonlinearly. For example, sometimes trust between two people begins at the surface level, where someone makes the decision that sustaining a particular relationship, even if it is difficult, is a better choice in that moment than severing it.[28] Some relationships stay at this level, where trust is seen only as a calculation of whether it is better to keep someone close or to let them go. In Shared Sisterhood, we suggest that people need to work to move from a calculus-based trust to a trust grounded in knowledge and predictability (in other words, I know and trust the person to act in certain ways) and in identification (that is, I identify with the other person's values and intentions). However, this result may not always occur. And sometimes trust is violated and you may move from a more identity-based trust back to one grounded in a calculation of benefits and costs. But understanding what trust is, why it's important, and how to work to improve it in your relationships is a critical component of Shared Sisterhood.

Risk-taking

The final core component of building authentic relationships within Shared Sisterhood is risk-taking—a linchpin component of authentic connection. Empathy can inspire risk-taking: without it, trust is difficult to maintain; within it, vulnerability is implied. When someone takes a risk, they risk their physical, social, or economic capital. People can make themselves vulnerable in interpersonal interactions and then choose to risk their relational capital on behalf of others. For example, making yourself vulnerable may mean sharing something about yourself that could lead you to be perceived as weak, racist, or insincere, putting your reputation at stake. Engaging in risk-taking means that you could lose your job, your friends, or your income. We characterize this as the difference between "What will people think of me?" versus "What will people do to me?"

One example of risk-taking stems from work on allyship. Professor Daniela Gachago wrote an essay on allyship in academia, noting that allyship is a verb—something you do.[29] She said, "It's taking risks, putting yourself on the line, asking uncomfortable questions" and not allowing business as usual to continue unabated. In her essay, she navigates between the constructs of vulnerability, empathy, and risk-taking, but her point about risk-taking is an apt one: you can't build a Sisterhood on words alone. At some point, you have to act on those words. And risk-taking is part of that action.

Each is necessary, but none is sufficient

There are limitations of each component of authentic connection. Each discrete component makes contributions to authentic connection and also has its own boundaries; if one of them is left out, the connections that people create will not be strong enough to promote collective action toward equity. Table 1-2 demonstrates what we mean: if we have connections that have vulnerability, trust, and empathy, but no risk-taking, then the likelihood of collective action is low, and the status quo will be maintained. Or, if we have risk-taking, trust, and empathy, but

TABLE 1-2

The necessity of all four components of authentic connection

Relational outcomes	Risk-taking present?	Vulnerability present?	Trust present?	Empathy present?
Inaction, maintain status quo	N	Y	Y	Y
Take action, but lack authentic connections for future actions	Y	N	Y	Y
Actions will not be trusted, difficult to proceed and connect with others (bridge)	Y	Y	N	Y
Actions not rooted in what the marginalized people may need	Y	Y	Y	N

no vulnerability in our interactions, we may lack the authenticity in our connection that can support future actions together.

It's also important to note the differences that emerge for women from historically marginalized versus historically dominant racio-ethnic groups (as we will do throughout the book). For instance, as a White woman, Beth may empathize with her Black colleague at work. Beth might work to make herself vulnerable as she uncovers her own biases and to build trust across differences. But if she does not pair this work with risk-taking on behalf of her Sister, the status quo may be maintained, limiting the ability to make real change toward collective action. Likewise, if Beth were to do all of the above, but failed to build trust with her colleague at work, the risks and actions that Beth takes may not be trusted. Her intentions will be questioned and bridging will be limited. In turn, Beth and her Black colleague will be limited in their ability to dismantle disparities in their jobs and realize collective action.

FIGURE 1-3

Tina's and Beth's different paths from Dig to Bridge

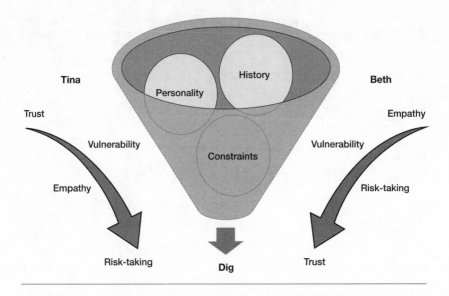

For Tina, as a Black woman, her journey may be different from Beth's. Due to collective history and Tina's personal experiences with betrayals, trust may be the most important place for Tina to begin when developing a relationship with a potential Shared Sisterhood partner. This may mean that trusting others, and making herself vulnerable to others, are her first necessary steps to build a bridge with a White woman at work, with empathy and risk-taking coming later (as shown in figure 1-3). These distinctions recognize collective power dynamics in the United States. When White women, and White people in general, demonstrate risk-taking on behalf of historically marginalized people, the risk they take can facilitate trust from historically marginalized people. Why? Because risk-taking means that the power-dominant person was willing to put their power to work to make power dynamics more equitable. As you practice Dig, where you surface and examine your assumptions and biases about racioethnicity, your unique background will affect the path you take toward building bridges with others.

Moving from the Individual to the Collective

While debate about women's workplace inequities has been raging for decades in the United States, Paula Abdul's iconic refrain "one step forward, two steps back" seems apropos when considering the pace of change in terms of pay equity (stalled), representation at the highest levels (also stalled), and even issues of sexual harassment (still controversial). We see that the longevity of the struggle has been a boon to many a bookstore self-help section, where women are encouraged to work on themselves, to invest in their skills, and to act with confidence and bravado to solve their workplace inequity problems. But if individual solutions that focused on individual women were all that was needed, why would gender inequity still persist?

Women's struggle for workplace equity has always been better understood through an intersectional lens. The term *intersectionality* was popularized by Professor Kimberlé Crenshaw, who pushed back on narrow definitions of discrimination in the law. Crenshaw implored legal scholars and practitioners to consider how the complex intersection of gender and racioethnicity affects ideas of justice under the law. Since her 1987 introduction of the term, it has gone mainstream, with Vox Media saying that the theory's "fundamental truth" is "that individuals have individual identities that intersect in ways that impact how they are viewed, understood, and treated."[30] Any effort to address gender inequity must thus also address the within-gender differences among women, racioethnicity being a particularly important difference to examine.

If women's workplace inequity is a collective problem that affects women as a group, then women as a group need to work collectively to solve it. The critical issue here, however, is that "women as a group" are composed of individual women, so we need an approach to help people learn how to work together to address workplace inequity. Successfully pursuing collective action toward equity thus requires that the Shared Sisterhood philosophy holistically address inequity across levels—from the individual, to the interpersonal, to the collective—in order to achieve our goals. We delve into the way these levels interact in chapter 2.

Thinking, Feeling, and Doing

Think

How were the core concepts of empathy, vulnerability, trust, and risk-taking evident in the story of Ida B. Wells-Barnett at the suffrage parade in 1913? What do you think the leaders of that parade could have done differently? This example focused on the historical relationships between Black and White women. If you are from a different racioethnic background, what historical stories come to mind that demonstrate interracial empathy, vulnerability, trust, and risk-taking? What historical stories illustrate the absence of these elements?

Feel

Consider Kim McLarin's statement (from the preface): "This is what Black women know: When push comes to shove, White women choose race over gender: Every. Single. Time." How did that line make you feel when you read it? Did you nod in agreement? Did you get a shiver of discomfort? If you are a woman of Hispanic/Latinx, Asian or Pacific Islander, or Native/Indigenous descent, can you relate to what McLarin wrote? Do you feel that White women choose racioethnicity over gender? How does that manifest in your specific racioethnic context?

Do

Consider one of your own interracial connections in the workplace. Using the core concepts of empathy, vulnerability, trust, and risk-taking, make your own checklist or table about what is present and what is missing in your relationship. Do you have empathy for one another? Have you taken risks? Repeat this exercise for other connections you have, or connections you want to have.

2

Sisterhood across Different Levels

I (Tina) was hired to conduct an enterprise-wide consulting project to help a large corporation address a problematic organizational culture. There were concerns about turnover and a lack of diversity at critical levels within the company. In our initial discussions, the company identified what seemed to be a clear organization-level problem. But, despite the system-level scope of the project, company leadership requested that I hold open meetings and/or office hours so that individual Black employees could receive coaching advice directly from me, rather than coaching organizational leaders on how to remove anti-Blackness from their recruiting, hiring, and performance-management systems. In my opinion, this approach would result in Black employees learning to perform better in an organization that was rife with anti-Blackness. I declined to continue the project.

One of the defining features and contributions of the Shared Sisterhood model is that it encompasses multiple levels of analysis, ranging from the individual (personal decisions, personality traits, and so forth), to the interpersonal (relationships between two people), to the collective (history, context, systems, and power dynamics within groups, organizations, or even societies). In our experience, the misunderstanding of levels is a central problem preventing collective action toward racioethnic and gender equity.

Often, we see people suggesting individual solutions when they confront structural problems—or vice versa. This leads to misunderstanding and an inability to move forward together. An example of ill-informed, incomplete, and harmful solutions due to a misdiagnosis of the level of a problem is reflected in a billboard that was constructed in various neighborhoods around the country. On the right side of the billboard we see a Black youth; "Proverbs 10:4" appears in the bottom right corner. On the left side of the billboard "Tired of Poverty?" is emblazoned above five points:

1. Finish School

2. Take Any Job

3. Get Married

4. Save and Invest

5. Give Back to Your Neighborhood

The five actions on the billboard are focused at the individual level, suggesting that the solution for Black poverty is for Black people to finish school, take any job, get married, save and invest, and give back to their neighborhoods. Those actions imply that if Black people acted with more agency, and pulled themselves up through education and work, poverty would be reduced. For those unfamiliar with Proverbs 10:4, the Bible verse quoted on the billboard, it reads "Lazy hands make for poverty, but diligent hands bring wealth" (New International Version)—suggesting that the creator of the billboard sees poverty as an individual problem needing individual solutions.

But this individual-level approach fails to address the structural issues that contribute to poverty: disparities in wages, health care, educational opportunities, policing, sentencing, hiring practices, and so on. Simultaneously, it places the blame on Black people for their plight while never mentioning historical factors including enslavement, Jim Crow, and racism that have contributed to contemporary racioethnic disparities. Proposing individual-level solutions to a broader problem can create barriers to actually solving the racial equity problem. If policy makers believe that individual-level solutions are the only necessary ingredient to resolve the poverty experienced by Black people, those same policy makers may fail to enact policies that address systemic issues. In this way, a misdiagnosis of levels can not only fail to solve a problem; it can make it worse.

This is a salient example, but far from the only one we have experienced. Accurately understanding at what level the crux of a problem lies is a critical first step to developing solutions. But, importantly, these complex issues of racioethnic and gender inequity often exist at multiple levels, which require multilevel solutions.

Our multilevel approach connects to a fundamental sociological theory, ecological systems theory, which explains that human behavior does not occur in a vacuum, and that relationships and contexts are important to understand how people function in the world. This theory argues that individual behaviors and outcomes are affected by, and in some cases dependent upon, the relationships and contexts in which they exist. This is a critical point, because directing solutions and recommendations at any one level risks oversimplifying a complex issue, leading to ineffective results or interventions that do more harm than good.

Critically, each level is necessary to address work inequities, but none is sufficient on its own. The goal of Shared Sisterhood is to promote collective action for all employees regardless of gender or racioethnicity. Collective action involves pay and promotion equity, fair and supportive work climates, and a lack of discrimination at work. But the process of Shared Sisterhood is also individual and interpersonal, focusing on creating organizational change via individual and interpersonal thought and action. All of these interactions and experiences are also nested in a historical context that is unique to the society in which the individual employees live and work.

Inspired by the nested models of ecological systems theory, figure 2-1 is a model of the nested levels of Shared Sisterhood. We describe each level of analysis and dive into an example on how misunderstanding levels of analysis can set us back.

There Are Levels to This

In our introduction of Shared Sisterhood as coalition building in *Organizational Dynamics*, we described the philosophy of Shared Sisterhood as moving from the individual to the interpersonal to the collective level built around two practices: Dig and Bridge.

Throughout this book we delve deeper into what we mean by Dig and Bridge and how readers can do both of these things. We are also clear about the levels that are being described. Is this an individual problem? If so, what are the individual solutions? And when

FIGURE 2-1

The nested levels of Shared Sisterhood

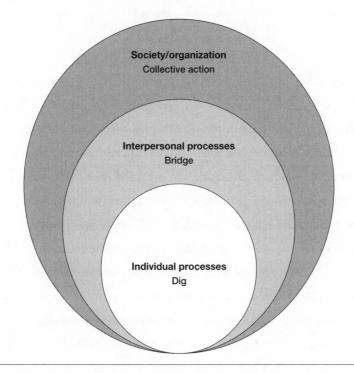

we discuss the interactions between levels, we talk about how they fit together and how that fit makes sense for you. As you read this book, you should be able to see how the problems and solutions we analyze sit at different levels, and even how research and history can obscure these issues in their attempt to simplify a complex, nuanced issue, so that you can see your own organizational reality more clearly. As in Tina's organizational consulting example at the beginning of this chapter, you will be able to understand when there is a mismatch between a problem and the solution that is being recommended to you (or even the solution that you are putting into action), and you will be able to use the practice of Dig and Bridge to find a path forward that is more likely to lead to collective action toward equity.

Individual

In research and common parlance, much of what we talk about when we talk about racism is really focused on individual people. How do we change what a person feels or thinks? How can I change how *I* feel or think? What could a person do differently to avoid a certain situation? All of these questions are centered on the individual level. In Shared Sisterhood, we account for the individual level via Dig, which promotes deep introspection and individual growth.

During the summer of 2020, in response to the murders of George Floyd in Minneapolis, Breonna Taylor in Kentucky, and Ahmaud Arbery in Georgia, many books on racioethnicity and racism sold out.[1] Individuals (often White women) bought books by the dozen: *How to Be an Antiracist*, by Ibram X Kendi; *So You Want to Talk about Race*, by Ijeoma Oluo; and *White Fragility*, by Robin DiAngelo, were three of the bestselling books of the year. Though many of these books acknowledge the limitations of a strictly individual-level approach to racioethnicity and racism, in some instances they were used as tools to help individual people combat racist ideas or behaviors. Much of the focus at that time, among that group, was on the individual: you can learn and work to change yourself.

Implicit bias research is based on this perspective as well. Research on implicit bias—the thought that people can act on prejudice without consciously meaning to—runs throughout education, law, psychology, health care, and business. It is also the focus of many training endeavors. An internet search of "implicit bias training" or "unconscious bias training" reveals hundreds, if not thousands, of websites

and organizations dedicated to training individuals on how to coun-
teract, or get rid of, their personal biases.

In fact, diversity, equity, and inclusion (DEI) approaches are sometimes denounced for overemphasizing this level, often because, as
Tina's example above demonstrates, individual solutions can feel easier for those in power (or with power) to enact or conceptualize.
Shifting focus from organizational to individual-level solutions is
endemic at many organizations. In fact, a recent *Harvard Business
Review* series articulated the limitations of a solely individual-based
approach.[2] The authors note that focusing on individual bias ignores
issues of interpersonal microaggressions and organizational culture
and power, thereby minimizing true organizational change. Shared
Sisterhood acknowledges the interpersonal and institutional issues
that contemporary approaches to DEI have underemphasized or
ignored, including changing interpersonal interactions or organizational structures.

Interpersonal

The connection between individual introspection and interpersonal
relationship building is captured in the Bridge component of Shared
Sisterhood, where two people seek authentic connections with one
another across differences. In research, we often talk about "dyads"
and relational interactions at work—but what this really means is that
there are two people making a connection. The interpersonal level
focuses on how two people, whether coworkers or friends, interact.

The interpersonal level was first highlighted in foundational work
by George Herbert Mead in *Mind, Self, and Society*. In this book, Mead
reflected on the three levels of analysis that operate when we interact
with the world via the mind (that is, understanding oneself), the self

(understanding oneself in the world, and perceptions of others), and society (the overall context in which people understand the world). The interpersonal level examines how individuals experience the self, based on their interpersonal interactions with other people. Likewise, when we consider the interpersonal level, we think about how two people communicate and experience the world together, for good or for bad.

An interpersonal lens can help us to understand experiences such as microaggressions. Microaggressions are commonplace, or even daily, experiences of what professor Derald Sue calls "verbal, behavioral, or environmental indignities, whether intentional or unintentional, that communicate hostile, derogatory, or negative racial slights and insults toward people of color."[3] These experiences cannot exist without at least two people: they are interpersonal by definition. Likewise, discrimination requires an actor and a target. This distinction between levels is important because when we focus on the individual level, debates about intent often arise. Did this person intend to make me feel this way? Individuals typically do not like to be labeled as discriminatory, so an egocentric, individualistic approach may lead to defensiveness and inhibit the ability to disentangle and improve upon the interpersonal interaction. In this way, an interpersonal focus can shift the conversation to how the discrimination affected the relationship between the two people. Interpersonal problems require different solutions than individual ones. In Shared Sisterhood, we acknowledge the necessity of both individual and interpersonal solutions to address the larger problems that contribute to collective inequity.

Collective

Inequity affects women and historically marginalized racioethnic people as a group or class that requires a collective-level solution. A collective level can include groups and teams within companies, the company or organization itself, and even neighborhoods, countries, or society at large. Wherever the focus is a group of people together, that is the collective level. Statistics about wages, labor force participation, and even the proportion of women CEOs at *Fortune* 500 companies, are all collective statistics that describe broad structural trends: they include individuals, who may have interpersonal connections, but the level addressed is the collective because we are attempting to understand at a wider level if our wages, recruiting processes, and so forth are equitable. Collective action among multiple individuals is a key metric to indicate the success of a Shared Sisterhood effort.

Shared Sisterhood contributes to organizational strategy, culture, leadership, and diversity literatures by addressing multiple levels simultaneously. In 2005 S. D. Dionne and her colleagues found that few studies discuss issues of levels theoretically, and even fewer analyze data at various levels.[4] Diversity and inclusion practitioners are beginning to talk about levels in important ways.[5] But in terms of solutions to real issues that real people experience at work, multiple levels are rarely considered. This is an important gap that helps to explain why organizational DEI efforts may not be as successful as we would like and why Shared Sisterhood is a helpful framework.

Prescribing Solutions at Multiple Levels

There's a saying that "if all you have is a hammer, everything is a nail." This is no less true for the researchers and managers who care about workplace inequities. If you typically see things as individual problems, then you will often continue to use an individual lens. If you are an economist, for instance, who examines societal or national trends, you will often continue to see problems of inequity using a country-level lens. The lenses you are comfortable with become your hammers.

But complex problems around inequality often require intervention and collaboration at multiple levels. In order to truly attack the systemic problems we face in both organizations and society, we need to be open to applying solutions at each level.

Pay equity in Hollywood across levels

The film industry offers many examples that illustrate these levels in action. Media mogul Shonda Rhimes and actress Ellen Pompeo, for instance, engaged in individual-level behaviors to redress pay inequity. Pompeo and Rhimes worked together for years on the medical drama *Grey's Anatomy*, with Pompeo as the longtime star of the show. As Rhimes gained more power in the production room, she empowered Pompeo to negotiate for what she deserved, and to do so as aggressively as the male stars do—to claim her power and worth.[6] So Pompeo did negotiate— one of the most popular individual-focused approaches to pay inequity.

The late actor Chadwick Boseman and actress Sienna Miller engaged in interpersonal behaviors to redress pay inequity. When Boseman and Miller were making the 2019 movie *21 Bridges*, Boseman realized that the studio was not going to pay Miller what she had asked for. Boseman then gave Miller part of his salary to convince her to sign on to the movie.[7] When Miller recounted this story in the wake of Boseman's 2020 death, she focused on his goodness and graciousness toward her, a very interpersonal perspective. And, indeed, Boseman's response to pay inequity was interpersonal: he reached out to a colleague and found a solution between the two of them.

Jessica Chastain and Octavia Spencer engaged in behaviors that reflect interpersonal and organizational behaviors to redress pay inequity. When Chastain and Spencer first spoke about pay inequity in Hollywood, Spencer alerted Chastain to the racial differences in pay that also exist. Chastain's reaction was both interpersonal ("I will advocate for you") but also collective: she started her own production company (organization) to combat this issue from an alternative position of power.[8] This is a collective approach to pay inequity.

All of these solutions address certain aspects of the problem, which is appropriate because the problem is multifaceted and exists at many different levels. But together these solutions are more likely to effectively dismantle workplace challenges such as pay inequity. We are seeing more continued discussion toward gender pay equity in Hollywood because of this combination of solutions rather than focus at any one level (see the sidebar "Moving beyond Pay in Hollywood").

Pay inequity at intersecting levels

Even outside of Hollywood, gender pay inequity is discussed this way. Economists and policy makers often talk about gender pay inequity at a structural level: in the United States, women make eighty-one cents to every dollar earned by a man, for example. In contrast, popular press articles, YouTube videos, and countless posts offer individual-level examples (such as "My female colleague makes more money than I do!") or provide potential solutions that address wage inequity at an individual level (such as "We need to teach women how to negotiate more assertively"). These individual anecdotes and solutions fail to capture the entirety of the issue and lead to inefficient and ineffective conversations and solutions.

Many organizational solutions function at the individual level: women are encouraged to negotiate and organizations offer classes for women to learn to be more assertive, to gain confidence, to ask

Moving beyond Pay in Hollywood

The Hollywood examples we've described not only involve gender pay inequity; they also reflect racioethnicity and racism. In fact, Octavia Spencer specifically drew Jessica Chastain's attention to the racial disparities that existed to divide women and prevent them from working together toward true equity. In chapter 4, we talk about how Chastain's reaction to this knowledge exhibited some of the hallmark qualities of Shared Sisterhood. For now, we focus on how racioethnic divisions could have prevented the collective solution to pay inequity that Chastain chose to employ by creating her own production company.

Chastain's first action was to link herself with Octavia Spencer to ensure that they were paid equally on projects they were on together. This is an interpersonal solution much like that which Chadwick Boseman used with Sienna Miller: band together and demand equity in contracts. Octavia Spencer described it as being a "most favored nation" when she worked with Chastain, and she described herself as making five times more in pay when Chastain followed through. Chastain's approach to overall pay inequity between men and women, however, was more structural: if existing production firms won't pay us equally, I'll create my own company (Freckle Films). What remains to be seen, however, is whether the same interracial collaboration in the name of equity that she employed with Spencer will be re-created at Freckle Films.

Director Ava DuVernay's approach to running her critically acclaimed show *Queen Sugar* provides another example of connection for collective action toward equity.[a] DuVernay expressly took risks to include Black women directors and writers who were not given opportunities that their White and male counterparts were given. She created a culture of belonging and inclusion that represented her vision, and she built in trust for what the women she chose could do, given the right resources. *Queen Sugar* actress Bianca Lawson said it perfectly: "Everyone is truly pulling each other up. Pushing each other forward, helping each other, it's not like mine and yours, but it's ours. It's a really hard thing to even describe. I can't believe that I'm witnessing it. I can't believe that I'm experiencing it. Powerful, intelligent women who are also passionate, but kind. There's a real warmth. There's a real feeling of sisterhood. You don't always get that. That's very rare."[b] This is a result of DuVernay using the structural power she earned to uplift and connect, eschewing an individually competitive approach in favor of collective action.

a. Lauren Alvarez, "How Ava DuVernay's *Queen Sugar* Is Pioneering a Movement of Inclusion, Representation in Television," Forbes.com, June 12, 2019, https://www.forbes.com/sites/laurenalvarez/2019/06/12/how-ava-duvernays-queen-sugar-is-pioneering-a-movement-of-inclusion-representation-in-television/?sh=525aa03a4302.

b. Alvarez, "How Ava DuVernay's *Queen Sugar* Is Pioneering."

for more. However, even if every woman engaged in these behaviors, we still might experience gender wage inequity. Why? Because, despite an individual's best negotiation skills, there are embedded systems that perpetuate wage inequity.

An individual may hone their negotiation skills but still be at a systemic disadvantage when compared to other individuals who are networked with people already in the organization. Thus, networks or structures become the differentiator more than negotiation skills.

Is it possible to network our way to gender equity? Doubtful. People are most likely to network with people who are similar to them. Again, networks reflect a system, a collective of individuals. People in power tend to network with others in power, to the exclusion of those with less power. Additionally, seemingly innocuous procedures may contribute to systemic inequities, such as the practice of employers asking for a job applicant's salary in prior roles. Given that women are paid less than men, this question systemically disadvantages women and historically marginalized members.

In table 2-1, we summarize some of the research on pay inequity based on different levels. The ideas in the table have been discussed in popular media and in the pages of the *New York Times*. Lay discussions about solving pay inequity often focus on individual-level solutions and overlook the challenges associated with enacting particular solutions. The table shows the level, an example of a solution proposed in the literature (many of which may seem familiar to you), an analysis of the problems with this solution, and, in the final column, how considering other levels may help fill in the gaps the proposed solution contains.[9]

For example, consider row 1, which suggests that individual women ought to exude self-confidence to address gender pay inequity at work. This seems like a very reasonable proposition, given that self-efficacy has been found to be positively related to pay and modesty negatively

TABLE 2-1

Pay equity solutions

Level	Solution	Why it's complicated	Other levels addressing the complications	Study
Individual	Exude confidence, self-efficacy	Acting outside the scope of a stereotype may result in agentic penalties	Societal gender norms, organizational culture	Robert W. Livingston, Ashleigh Shelby Rosette, and Ella F. Washington, "Can an Agentic Black Woman Get Ahead? The Impact of Race and Interpersonal Dominance on Perceptions of Female Leaders," *Psychological Science* 23, no. 4 (2012): 354–358. Ashleigh Shelby Rosette, Christy Zhou Koval, Anyi Ma, and Robert Livingston, "Race Matters for Women Leaders: Intersectional Effects on Agentic Deficiencies and Penalties," *Leadership Quarterly* 27, no. 3 (2016): 429–445.
Individual	Stand up for yourself	If you stand up, you might be perceived as overly aggressive	Societal gender norms, organizational culture	D. R. Forsyth, M. M. Heiney, and S. S. Wright, "Biases in Appraisals of Women Leaders," *Group Dynamics: Theory, Research, and Practice* 1, no. 1 (1997): 98–103, https://doi.org/10.1037/1089-2699.1.1.98. Victoria L. Brescoll and Eric Luis Uhlmann, "Can an Angry Woman Get Ahead? Status Conferral, Gender, and Expression of Emotion in the Workplace," *Psychological Science* 19, no. 3 (2008): 268–275.
Interpersonal	Negotiate with your boss	If you negotiate, you are penalized	Societal gender norms	Maria Recalde and Lise Vesterlund, "Gender Differences in Negotiation and Policy for Improvement," working paper 28183, National Bureau of Economic Research, 2020, https://www.nber.org/papers/w28183. "Counteracting Negotiation Biases Like Race and Gender in the Workplace," Program on Negotiation, Harvard Law School, November 19, 2020, https://www.pon.harvard.edu/daily/leadership-skills-daily/counteracting-racial-and-gender-bias-in-job-negotiations-nb/. Morela Hernandez, Derek R. Avery, Sabrina D. Volpone, and Cheryl R. Kaiser, "Bargaining While Black: The Role of Race in Salary Negotiations," *Journal of Applied Psychology* 104, no. 4 (2019): 581. Benjamin Artz, Amanda Goodall, and Andrew J. Oswald, "Research: Women Ask for Raises as Often as Men, but Are Less Likely to Get Them," hbr.org, June 25, 2018, https://hbr.org/2018/06/research-women-ask-for-raises-as-often-as-men-but-are-less-likely-to-get-them.

(continued)

TABLE 2-1 (continued)

Pay equity solutions

Level	Solution	Why it's complicated	Other levels addressing the complications	Study
Interpersonal	Bargain together with other women	Gender discrimination in union organization makes this hard	Organizational norms (in unions)	Charlotte Yates, "Challenging Misconceptions about Organizing Women into Unions," *Gender, Work, and Organization* 13, no. 6 (2006): 565–584.
Organizational	Diversify boards of directors and leadership roles	Ensuring baseline levels of gender representation does not always work	Individual feelings of being left out, societal gender norms	Stacey R. Fitzsimmons, "Women on Boards of Directors: Why Skirts in Seats Aren't Enough," *Business Horizons* 55, no. 6 (2012): 557–566.
				Ann L. Owen and Judit Temesvary, "CEO Compensation, Pay Inequality, and the Gender Diversity of Bank Board of Directors," *Finance Research Letters* 30 (2019): 276–279.
Organizational	Remove firms' incentive to disproportionately reward workers who work long, particular hours	Societal drivers of the gap are still present	Societal gender norms, relational interactions with spouse/partner	Francine D. Blau and Lawrence M. Kahn, "The Gender Wage Gap: Extent, Trends, and Explanations," *Journal of Economic Literature* 55, no. 3 (2017): 789–865.
				Nikke Graf, Anna Brown, and Eileen Patten, "The Narrowing, but Persistent, Gender Gap in Pay," Pew Research Center, April 9, 2018, https://leametz. pbworks.com/f/Gender%20pay%20gap%20has%20narrowed%2C%20 but%20changed%20little%20in%20past%20decade.pdf.
Societal	Increase education opportunities	Much of the gap remains unexplained	Organizational culture toward what they value/ compensate at work	Christianne Corbett and Catherine Hill, *Graduating to a Pay Gap: The Earnings of Women and Men One Year after College Graduation* (Washington, DC: American Association of University Women, 2012), https://eric.ed.gov/?id=ED536572.
Societal	Lobby for parental leave	Individuals who take leave, even when available, can face backlash	Organizational culture	Matthew B. Perrigino, Benjamin B. Dunford, and Kelly Schwind Wilson, "Work-Family Backlash: The 'Dark Side' of Work-Life Balance (WLB) Policies," *Academy of Management Annals* 12, no. 2 (2018): 600–630.

related to pay. But research has also suggested that when women act in bold, confident, agentic ways, they can incur backlash in the form of pay and promotion penalties for not conforming to stereotypes of normative femininity, and those norms can exist societally across cultures but also organizationally across companies. Thus, as shown in the final column, this individual-level solution is complicated by societal gender norms and organizational-level norms as well.

Bridging Divides across Levels

Hollywood makes for easy examples. The actors are household names, and we can picture the work they do and see how similar it is across the industry. It makes pay equity conversations simpler. But in complex, opaque organizations, we may not have agents representing multiple actors to compare salaries, or easy-to-define work that makes it clear that what is happening is unfair. And, though the racioethnic disparities within gender groups still are apparent, individual and interpersonal solutions can occur because of the tight-knit working relationships that many actors have. One Jessica Chastain can wield a lot of power. So could one Chadwick Boseman. Many of us outside of Hollywood don't have such power, and we may therefore feel disempowered to make significant change. So how can regular employees band together toward collective action? How can they reckon with racial and gender differences so that everyone can win?

One woman whom we will call Sarah was charged with improving gender equity at her male-dominated firm. Women in leadership were few and far between. Sarah diligently focused on increasing gender equity but realized that she did not have deep knowledge when it came to combating racism. Sarah wanted to learn how to take an intersectional approach so that she could address both gender and racioethnic inequities, so she reached out to Black, Asian, and Hispanic women colleagues to learn more. During these interactions, Sarah realized that her women colleagues from historically marginalized racioethnic groups were having different experiences than she was. Sarah was curious. She developed closer, authentic interpersonal connections across racioethnic lines, and she built on those relationships. These connections paved the way to increasing the number of women in particular position pipelines, particularly women of color—all of whom she supported and elevated. Sarah could have solely focused on gender equity and overlooked racioethnic equity, but she integrated the two and created real change.

Throughout our work as researchers, teachers, and consultants, we have seen these real struggles happening in organizations across industries. For instance, consider a White woman, a middle-level manager who asks for personal coaching advice to help be a better manager and advocate for the women of color she works with, who is seeking an individual solution because that is all that she feels that she can control. Yet, this manager could dig a bit deeper and focus on her hiring and recruiting procedures and analyze pay tables by racioethnicity and gender. We help her to identify her fears and concerns and identify what she *can* do across levels. Or, consider a White executive, who, upon seeing the metrics on racioethnicity and gender and promotion in his company, asks for help to create the needed cultural change to make Shared Sisterhood possible. This executive could also involve the rest of his executive team so that the information has a better chance of changing the organizational culture. Or, consider members of a Women's Interest Group who want to create real change for women in their company across racioethnic lines, who learn how to have difficult but authentic conversations to lay the foundation for their collective action. The solutions they seek range across levels, from individual to interpersonal to organizational, and they work in industries ranging from finance to education, from entertainment to manufacturing. But they have one thing in common: they want to effect change.

Shared Sisterhood is a way to bridge these divides across levels. This may seem naive: after all, these divides have existed for hundreds of years. These same kinds of divides made it difficult for women like Belle Squire and Ida B. Wells-Barnett to advocate for women as a collective group. What can the paradigm of Shared Sisterhood do that has not been done before? Our argument is this: Many solutions that have been tried in organizations are myopic. Individuals are trained or lectured. Systems may be audited, but they are rarely adjusted. Multilevel solutions are rarely attempted. Shared Sisterhood leverages authentic connections to radically reimagine and change structures to achieve equity across levels. It does not argue for mere representation, a numerical diversity that does not lead to collective action for the whole. It argues for changing how people think about themselves and others, how they interrelate with colleagues at work, and what organizations reward or penalize.

In chapters 3 and 4 we use the philosophy of Shared Sisterhood and the practices of Dig and Bridge to discuss the importance of authentic connections in an organizational context. We start with Dig, which sits primarily at the individual level, by interrogating our own biases and assumptions: Are we being a hammer when what we need is a nail? Some have argued that efforts for DEI need not address the hearts and minds of organizational leaders, as the important focus should be on policies and procedures. Our approach contends that it is very difficult to lead collective action toward equity on issues with which you have little, if any, personal connection, insight, or conviction to change. What if organizational policies and procedures could be best influenced and created by individuals who have personal understanding of and connection to their own racio-ethnic identity? This is why we start with Dig, even though we must not end there.

Thinking, Feeling, and Doing

Think

Think about what you did to create change in the wake of the murder of George Floyd in 2020. What level were you thinking about at that time? Yourself? Your interpersonal relationships? Society as a whole?

Feel

Imagine you were a woman concerned that you were not being paid fairly compared to a male counterpart. Perhaps you noted that many women had left promising positions in the company in the past few quarters. How would you feel if your colleague suggested that you take negotiation training courses to solve this problem? What emotions would you experience?

Do

Consider a problem you have faced related to diversity, equity, and inclusion. It could be related to pay, promotion, or how you (or a colleague) are treated. Write down what you've done to address this and note whether they were actions/solutions aimed at the individual, interpersonal, or collective level. What more could you have done? Has the problem been solved? If not, what other levels can you use to do more?

3

Digging into Dig

D ig is a practice designed to help you surface your assumptions about racioethnicity and understand how those assumptions frame your perceptions of racioethnicity in the world. It is focused on your individual assumptions, emotions, thoughts, and perceptions about racioethnicity, which are likely informed by the contexts in which you were born, raised, and have lived. While doing your own Dig work, examining your emotions may lead you to uncover that there are systemic issues that have contributed to how you think and feel. Dig is a constant practice because our assumptions and perceptions may shift as we grow and experience different people, workplaces, and contexts. Below we share some of our own Dig journeys.

As I (Beth) shared in the preface, when I entered college, I had more of a journey to take to understand the construction of racism around me. I remember taking a class called Whiteness and Racism, which was one of the first times that I had thought about my own racioethnicity and what it meant to be White, particularly as a White girl living in Kentucky. The class was set up almost as an exercise in Dig, where we would read and talk about how the books and articles made us feel about the world we live in. It was a place where I could reckon with what I felt while thinking through my role in perpetuating Whiteness and racism in my own life, and how I would work to dismantle it. When had I sat back and said nothing when someone made a racist joke? When should I have worked harder to prove myself trustworthy in relationships with people whose racioethnicity was different from my own? I had been raised with so many Black young people in my life, whom I loved, but did I really understand how our lives were different? It was through this process of Dig that I started to understand the intersections of racioethnicity and power for the first time.

In contrast to Beth's story, I (Tina) have been thinking about my racioethnicity and related power dynamics since I was a little girl. My parents surrounded us with examples of Black excellence out of pride in our heritage, but also as a proactive step to buffer us against the anti-Black racism that swirled around outside the doors to our home. For example, my parents had to explain racism to me when I got into the pool and all the White children got out; when my seventh grade algebra teacher refused to call on me, asserted that I didn't belong in the gifted and talented program, and attempted to grade me lower than my scores indicated (my mother took care of that). From an early age, racioethnicity and power dynamics were made apparent to me at multiple levels of analysis: at the individual, interpersonal, and collective levels it was clear that I was Black and that I was perceived as being a member of a collective known as Black people. Thus, my personal and social identities were connected to my Blackness.

The contrast between when Tina learned about being Black and the power dynamics of anti-Blackness (as a young child) and when

Beth learned about being White and the power dynamics of Whiteness (as a college student) is striking. And this significant difference
in timing also affects workplace interactions: Black people may be far
more advanced in their understanding of racioethnicity and power
dynamics than their White counterparts, a difference that affects
their Dig journeys. Research on social identity and power help us
understand the connection between how we identify, how others
perceive our identities, and how we navigate the racialized world
around us.

When did you begin to understand racism and power? Which of
our experiences is more similar to your own? Why might that be?
These moments of reflection are great entry points to the Dig process, particularly when they help us understand our own identities
and the power structure that surrounds them.

The Historical Relationship between
Social Identity and Power

This gap in knowledge and lived experience begins to explain why
workplace conversations about racioethnicity fall short of anticipated
progress toward diversity, equity, and inclusion; it also demonstrates
a critical component of the Dig practice: unearthing assumptions
that people have about the social identities that they hold.

Social identity theory describes how individuals understand themselves as creatures within a world that includes many different groups
with various characteristics.[1] A social identity is the part of a person's
sense of self that comes from being a part of a group and the emotions
that are attached to that sense of self.[2] We all have personal identities
(like "nice" or "smart") and social identities that are associated with

groups (such as gender, racioethnicity, sports team, religion, political affiliation, and so forth). Those identities can be weaker or stronger across people, and even change within people. For instance, we could generally know that, yes, we are women, but how we feel about our "woman identity" may shift and change and become more or less salient if we are the only women in the room, or one of hundreds. The Dig practice is directly affected by each specific social identity and the power dynamics associated with that identity. Importantly, each of us holds multiple identities, some imbued with social power that are dominant in the culture (for instance, Beth is White) while simultaneously holding identities that have been historically marginalized (for instance, Beth is a woman). The Dig practice differs for people with power-dominant identities versus people with historically marginalized identities because membership in power-dominant identities may blind us to specific ways in which we need to dig.

In Dig, we ask people to uncover their own social identities and the distinctive features of the groups they are associated with—but also to understand how those identities are situated in a broader social context of history, status, and power. The determination of how our social identities are associated with status and power is a critical component of Dig because it determines how people in groups may navigate their identities and their relationships with others both within and outside of their social groups, and it affects the norms and biases that a person may need to understand and navigate to be able to bridge. For example, people in historically marginalized groups may redefine their group membership by focusing on positive dimensions of group comparison, like the Black is Beautiful movement in the 1960s.[3] Research on ethnic identity follows this strategy, demonstrating that those from historically marginalized groups with stronger positive ethnic identities may be able to navigate discrimination and bias with less negative long-term psychological effects.[4]

But, as we noted in our own Dig stories, ethnic identity development may differ based on your racioethnic group. Remember Tina's story about learning about her Blackness at an early age versus Beth's story about learning about her Whiteness in college? Empirical research comparing ethnic identity development for Black and White college students corroborates this pattern. As they engaged in the process of understanding their identities, White and Black adolescents echoed the experiences of Beth's and Tina's Dig journeys, respectively—Black teens spoke to their families about what it meant to be Black and about future prejudice they may encounter.[5] In contrast, when White adolescents spoke to their families about racioethnicity and ethnicity, it was rarely about the construction of their own Whiteness, focusing instead on the racioethnicity of historically marginalized others. These differences mean that this chapter will affect readers differently, based on the social identities they hold.

The difference in Dig journeys is based on one's social identities and the power associated with those identities. Although this book focuses on racioethnicity and gender, there are other identities that are imbued with power, and examining these identities helps to underscore how Dig works. Religion is one such identity and, in the United States, Christianity is the dominant religious social identity. As a result, if Christians want to eliminate religious-based inequities, they have to proactively examine the Christian faith to understand how it might be affecting people outside of the faith. Why? Because Christianity is normative in the United States and, like the air we breathe, the effects of Christian norms often go unnoticed by members of the Christian faith. For example, when reviewing the academic calendar, it was only when I (Tina) was older that I contended with the fact that while schools are closed for Christmas holidays, they are often not closed for Jewish, Muslim, or Hindu holidays. Was I actively anti-Jewish or anti-Muslim? No. But, my membership in a dominant religious group blinded me in some ways to how members of historically marginalized religious groups were disadvantaged. Christian people living in societies that privilege a Christian identity have to actively interrogate Christian norms in order to avoid disadvantaging people from other religious backgrounds. Further, once I became aware of the religious calendar discrepancy, it was incumbent upon me to speak up from my relatively privileged position when I observed policies and procedures that replicated the systemic inequities. Further, I committed to the Dig practice by continuously educating myself and actively interrogating the norms associated with my Christian faith.

Interrogating one's own beliefs and the norms and status associated with those beliefs is a critical part of the Dig practice. In the specific case of racioethnicity, we encourage White people to interrogate their fundamental beliefs about racism and power dynamics, given that the social identity of "White" is a historically dominant social identity that has been associated with power and status in the United States. But it is important to note that the Dig practice is not just about self-reflection for its own sake. That reflection should lead to important questions you ask yourself about your identities, your interpersonal relationships and biases, and the ways in which your identities are associated with power and status. Truly understanding yourself is a critical first step in Shared Sisterhood. Without knowledge of the self, it is difficult to forge authentic connection and take collective action to dismantle systems of inequity.

Critical Steps to the Dig Practice

We have constructed a series of steps and questions to help you work through the process of learning about your social identities and how they fit into societal structures of power.

Identify who you are

First, identify your social identities and how much you identify with each of them. When we do this exercise in workshops, we often have a worksheet with various spaces for participants to record their identities. You might include "woman" or "man" or "nonbinary." Or "Hispanic" or "Black" or "Chinese." You may also include identities like "Christian" or "Southerner" or even "fan of your favorite sports team." Please be honest and write down what you actually think at this moment. Then think about which of those identities are most central to who you think you are. This will vary from person to person.

Research power dynamics

Next, research power and historical marginalization of each identity. As we noted above, each social identity has a different relationship to status and power. And many of us are members of various groups of various levels of status in our society. This step is critical because it is often missing from the introspection that individuals can sometimes engage in as they learn about their own identities. But understanding power is a nonnegotiable component of Dig.

- *For members of historically power-dominant groups:* Ask yourself what other groups have been marginalized by your collective group. How? Why? Really think about the ways in which members of your group have benefited from, and replicated, the power dynamics that you experience today—individually, interpersonally, and institutionally. You may find yourself resisting this question (for example, telling yourself that "my identity has never benefited me. I've had to work hard for everything that I've gotten"). If so, take a few moments and ask, "What if my identity has benefited me, and others with different identities have been harmed?" I may have worked hard or had difficulties, but was it because of this particular identity? Pay attention to how this makes you feel and what this makes you think.

- *For members of historically marginalized groups:* Ask yourself what other groups have been privileged by your group's historical marginalization. How? Why? Really think about the ways in which members of your group have experienced the ramifications of the power dynamics that exist today—individually, interpersonally, and institutionally. Pay particular attention to how this makes you feel and what this makes you think.

Recognize knowledge gaps

Often, people from privileged groups benefit from proactively seeking information to educate themselves about power dynamics related to their group. The story about Christian social identities above comes from Tina's lived experience reckoning with how Christian people may have done grave harm to others in the name of the Christian faith. Knowledge gaps are almost inevitable and are a part of the learning process. The need to learn is nothing to be ashamed of. Taking a learning orientation toward your discoveries can help you to focus on the future instead of the past—but it is critical that when you dig up a knowledge gap, you do not rest on your laurels; you must work to close it.

You need to understand the common responses to knowledge gaps in order to make sure that you react in a way that promotes growth and not stagnation. Research has suggested that White people often have three primary responses to learning about the power and privilege associated with their social (racial) identity: they can deny and refute the existence of their relative power, they can work to psychologically detach or distance themselves from their White identity to show that they "aren't like those White people," or they can work to eliminate systems of inequity that privilege their group over other racioethnicities.[6] Obviously, we hope that many of our readers will react to dismantle the systems that grant such power to certain racioethnic groups and not others. But our experience suggests that is not always the case. Here are the responses we often see to knowledge gaps that emerge:

Deny the existence of issues related to racioethnicity and power dynamics. It can be appealing to deny that you have a knowledge or experience gap, or to deny the existence of White privilege or racioethnic disparities. This denial often occurs when a revelation is unexpected or newly discovered. Recognizing this response is important because it can be a signal that you should listen more to others or go back to the first step above and dig more deeply.

Become defensive. White people can also have defensive reactions to learning about racioethnic power dynamics. For example, rather than focusing on the power dynamics of social identities that they have, they focus on blaming others for their ignorance; saying "It's not my fault that I didn't know" is a common defensive reaction. Another defensive reaction is to denigrate those from historically marginalized groups as unworthy so that any disparities that were uncovered during Dig can be blamed on the "other group." Part of the Dig practice is to be honest about any defensiveness you feel. Each emotional reaction is a signal and a cue. It doesn't feel good to have us, or anyone, point out that your life perceptions or worldview might be biased in some way, or that you may hold identities that are associated with status and power in ways you did not know or understand. However, when we dig, we must acknowledge our defensiveness and, rather than allowing it to alter the course of the discussion, we examine it. We interrogate ourselves by asking: Why am I defensive? What did I just read that made me feel this way? What emotions am I feeling right now? What am I thinking? And, finally, if you are having difficulty with this response, you might ask yourself, "Even if I *think* they are wrong, what if what Beth and Tina are saying is true?" Thinking about the counterfactual is sometimes an easier way to engage in growth-related thinking, particularly if you use that possibility to imagine how your perspective, attitudes, or behaviors would change if you were wrong.

Downplay discussions about racism by embracing color blindness. This is another very common reaction that we see when we talk about Dig. We understand the desire to say that one is color-blind. In the most positive sense, saying, "I don't see color" is an attempt to say that we are all human, that you value people because of who they are, not something as surface level and inconsequential as skin color. It is associated with a humanist ideology that attempts to disregard differences.[7] But herein lies the problem: Given what we know about racioethnic power dynamics, *is* skin color inconsequential in the society in which we live? While we might wish it to be so, history and contemporary lived experience speak to how skin color has substantially influenced the course of historical and contemporary life. As a Black woman, I (Tina) have said, "Listen, if we could go back to the beginning of time and make it so that people appreciated skin color differences as we appreciate differences in flower colors, that would be great. If we could get rid of the social construct of racioethnicity and focus on individuals, that could be awesome. But we do not live in that world. Plus, I am proud of being Black. What needs to change is not my Blackness but your devaluation of my Blackness."

Historically, people in society have used the social construct of racioethnicity to build real barriers based on that racioethnicity, creating institutional, interpersonal, and individual roadblocks to connection. However, this means that the abolishment of the social construct of racioethnicity would not lead to the abolishment of racioethnic disparities and racism. In fact, if the term *racioethnicity* was banished, it would make it difficult to describe the pernicious differences between racioethnic people groups, or to understand the power structures associated with social identities that we asked you to think about. In essence, while the notion of color blindness may have innocuous intentions, in application color-blind really means *power*-blind because a false perception that color doesn't or shouldn't matter to us for human interaction mutes us and blinds us to real power dynamics that oppress Black people and members of other historically marginalized racioethnic groups. This blindness prevents us from acknowledging and closing knowledge gaps, and thus prevents us from the authentic connections we aim for in Shared Sisterhood. Reflecting upon your own blind spots and knowledge gaps can help facilitate the Dig practice.

Common Questions for Dig

Below is a summary of common issues that come up when people engage in the Dig practice. Consider thinking about these questions as you go through the practice. Additionally, this list is something that you might want to share with others as they join you on the Dig journey.

1. When learning about your own racioethnic identity and other social identities, consider how much time you have committed to understanding racioethnic groups other than your own. How relevant do you believe that their racioethnicity is to their lives? What factors led you to answer the way that you did?

2. When you conduct historical research and reading into your own racioethnicity and social identities, how do you feel? What do you think? To what extent do you agree or disagree with what you have discovered? Consider the most important things you have learned about your group and what this means for what you know about yourself.

3. Think about how you feel when you hear statistics about racioethnic disparities (such as crime levels, educational attainment, economic gain, and so forth). If you are a dominant group member, do you experience a feeling of superiority based on your racioethnicity? Or, if you are a member of a historically marginalized racioethnic group, do you experience a feeling of inferiority? For example, perhaps you may think that certain racioethnic groups lack cultural values, leading to poorer outcomes. Examine your initial feelings and thoughts.

Emotions as Cues to Dig

Once you have identified your identities and how they are associated with various levels of power and status, you can learn to use your emotions as signals for your need to dig. Feelings of anger, guilt, frustration, fear—all of these are real, authentic, and valid. But they are also signals for you to investigate—and sometimes interrogate—yourself. In our experience, one of the most common emotions that White people experience in regard to connecting with people who are different from them is fear of being labeled as racist, incompetent, or ignorant. On the other hand, one of the most common emotions that historically marginalized people often have regarding these same interactions is the fear of being racially traumatized or threatened physically and emotionally. While the emotion of fear itself may ostensibly be the same, its cause—and thus its effects—are different for Black and White women like ourselves. Dig is a critical tool to uncover the source of such emotions, and it can be a tool to help you to work through the preconceptions and experiences that you have had to determine whether you are ready to build authentic bridges with people of different racioethnicities than your own.

Exploring White women's fear of being seen as racist

Confronting those fears using Dig can take courage, and there are different implications for Black and for White women who do so. Glennon Doyle, an author and podcast host, offers a great example for White women to learn how to identify situations that may require Dig and demonstrates how to make a healthy course correction that focuses attention on members of historically marginalized groups. In Doyle's memoir *Untamed*, she spoke about a time when she was asked to host and organize a webinar to teach White women about racism and how to dismantle racism. Figure 3-1 shows Doyle's original post and an update from 2018.

The news that she was going to host a webinar for White women on racism was met with excitement but also backlash. For example, comments on her social media posts included one from a Black woman who said, "Our voices need to be amplified, listened to, heard AND changes need to be made accordingly." Another back-and-forth in the comments involved a White woman who said, "Why can't we (white women) follow Black women?" noting that Doyle was not an expert on racism and should perhaps promote Black women's voices instead. Doyle responded to this comment, noting that Black women directly asked her to help White women to unlearn racism, which the webinar was intended to do. Other comments asked her to consider who is put into the spotlight with such an event.

In her book she also talks about her emotional reaction to this (unexpected) backlash to her post. She writes, "Friendly fire was new and excruciating. I felt idiotic and remorseful. I also felt terribly jealous of every single person who had decided to sit this one out. I thought of the quote 'It is better to be quiet and thought a fool than to open your mouth and prove it.' I felt defensive, hurt, frustrated, and afraid. I could not think of a single thing I was more terrified of being called than a racist. This was rock bottom."[8] But Doyle then exemplifies Dig because those emotions did not paralyze her. Rather, she used her emotions as cues for what actions she needed to take.

What does she uncover in that moment using her Dig skills? That she does not know everything yet—and that she is still unlearning a lot of racism. She listened to the criticism she received from people she trusted, particularly Black women who had

FIGURE 3-1

Glennon Doyle's post about moderating a discussion on race

Glennon Doyle

UPDATE to those asking the very valid question as to why two white women are moderating this discussion for white women about race in America:

I am a part of a group called #BlackFridays, which is a movement founded by and led by women of color. In a meeting recently, those leaders told me that what they wanted and needed me to do- as a white activist in the group- is to help other white women learn, take risks, and have hard conversations. My job in the context of this work is the listen to and follow the lead of Black womxn, and this webinar was created at the direct request of the women of color to whom I am holding myself accountable. I will not post their names here -- as I have not asked their permission to send thousands of white women their way. It is not the responsibility and burden of Black women to do the labor of educating white women. If you care to learn more about the #BlackFridays mission, or the women of color leading it- please go to our websites here:

https://actionnetwork.org/forms/blackfridays-we-do-not-consent

https://docs.google.com/document/d/1Qm7bGMAS-TPq-BsDMXhq0oElzz9keN qlX6_O-ICLNiU/edit

https://actionnetwork.org/event_campaigns/on-blackfridays-we-refuse-to-comply

https://secure.actblue.com/donate/blackfridays

Original Post:
HELLO FRIENDS!! Questions for you:

1. Are you a white woman?
2. Are you confused about your place in the race conversation?
3. Are you interested in taking the first step toward getting involved in racial justice work?
4. Are you interested in learning about how to have awkward, helpful conversations with friends and family about race?
5. Do you feel overwhelmed by all the things you *could* do and unclear of what you *should* do?

JOIN ME AND HEATHER (wonderful warrior from Showing Up for Racial Justice (SURJ)) -- tomorrow night Nov 1 at 8 PM ET -- for a conversation on white women and race in America. This is a free webinar for women brand-new to the race conversation -- our intention is to provide a space to ask questions, listen and learn, find purposeful community, and link up with some current efforts to make these conversations real. REGISTER (for free) here: http://bit.ly/WhiteWomenShowingUp

#BlackFridays

Source: Glennon Doyle, "Update to Those Asking the Very Valid Question as to Why Two White Women Are Moderating This Discussion for White Women about Race in America," October 31, 2018, https://m .facebook.com/glennondoyle/photos/update-to-those-asking-the-very-valid-question-as-to-why-two -white-women-are-mod/10156777421289710/. Reproduced by permission.

pushed back against her (well-intentioned) actions. Doyle had positive intentions when organizing the event; her prior actions and solidarity with Black organizers corroborate her positive intent. Yet, recall that intent is not how we determine if we are engaging in Shared Sisterhood; rather, we must understand the impact that our actions have on the marginalized group members we are attempting to aid.

The next day, Doyle made another post on social media, explaining why she decided to do the webinar in the first place, and why she decided to cancel it. She specifically noted that she had caused hurt and harm, and she was careful to emphasize the voices of specific women of color who had provided that feedback to her. She apologized, stated that she was listening and learning, and promised to do better. She also directed her followers to donate their money to a specific anti-racist action fund created and led by Black and Brown women.

Doyle's words and actions are powerful because, rather than engaging in denial, distancing, defensiveness, or embracing a color-blind ideology, she used the negative feedback to continue the Dig process. Doyle spoke of herself and other White women who are working to be allies against racism in her book: "She will have to accept that one of the privileges she's letting burn is her emotional comfort. She will need to remind herself that being called a racist is actually not the worst thing. The worst thing is privately hiding her racism to stay safe, liked, and comfortable while others suffer and die. There are worse things than being criticized—like being a coward."[9] Doyle role-modeled how to use negative feedback and emotional discomfort to fuel rather than stall growth, and she has continued her commitment to Dig as evidenced by her posts and podcasts that reflect a commitment to racioethnic equity.

Through our individual experiences and exposure gained during Shared Sisterhood group discussions on Facebook and Clubhouse, we have learned that many people from historically dominant groups cite fear of backlash as a key reason that they avoid attempting collective equity work or bridging with others. Members of historically power-dominant groups recount a surprisingly similar sequence of events when describing prior attempts to respond to racism or inequity or attempts to connect with people across racio-ethnic difference:

1. They craft a well-intentioned response to racism or inequity, or an attempt to help someone from a historically marginalized collective.

2. They receive criticism or backlash that they did not anticipate. They assumed that their positive intent would be clear to others.

3. They feel negative emotions, like frustration, defensiveness, or fear, in response to how others are responding to them and their efforts.

As a historically dominant group member, once you experience these negative emotions, you have a choice. Will you react by closing yourself off from those emotions? Will you remain defensive and defiant? Or will you let Doyle's experience be a guide and use those emotions as a cue for your own growth? As a cue to help you repair harm that you may have done to members of historically marginalized groups? If you choose to grow and repair, Dig is the skill set and the tool that can help you do better as you know better. And it can help you to grow into a person who is ready and able to authentically connect with people who are different from yourself.

Black women explore racial trauma

As a Black woman, I (Tina) have experienced racial trauma at work, and these experiences make me wary of White women colleagues who in one breath talk about feminism and gender equity, but in the next breath deny the existence of racism, take credit for my ideas, counsel me to be "more professional" by being less Afrocentric, encourage me to remain silent in the face of injustice, tell me that I am intimidating and angry, offer unsolicited advice on my hair (or ask to touch my hair), share resources with each other but fail to share them with me, denigrate my ideas, and much more. Additionally, I have watched White women exclude me from workplace lunches, forget to invite me to dinners, champion policies that promote gender equity but fail to mention racioethnic issues, remain silent when other colleagues cast aspersions on efforts to increase diversity, equity, and inclusion, and privately offer support after remaining silent in public. To cope, I developed defense mechanisms to protect myself, an armor of sorts. The challenge is that armor can prevent necessary sunlight, air, and connection.

With this backdrop, Dig practice helped me understand my emotional reactions to Beth when she first reached out to me. I didn't trust her and was hesitant to engage. Dig led me to ask myself questions like, "Why don't you trust Beth? Has she given you any evidence that she is not trustworthy? If not, what is going on? Why aren't you opening up to her?" While I needed to dig for reasons different than those that motivated Glennon Doyle, a common thread is that Dig was initiated by emotions as a cue to spur a process of self-discovery in which I asked myself questions and honestly considered the answers to them. What is different is the impetus for the process—the cause of the emotions, the emotions themselves, and the power dynamics derived from the current and historical context are vastly different. And as we demonstrated in the anecdotes we shared early in this chapter, power associated with our social identities (and when we are made aware of it) is critical to how Dig occurs.

Author bell hooks alludes to what Dig might look like for women of color, stating: "Women of color must confront our absorption of white supremacist beliefs, internalized racism, which may lead us to feel self-hate, to vent anger and rage at injustice at one another rather than at oppressive forces."[10] hooks describes how racialized trauma may lead people from historically marginalized racioethnic groups to distrust members of dominant racioethnic groups. This distrust may be the result of lived experiences and history and hence serves as an adaptive response to systems of oppression. Yet, this distrust may also prevent authentic connection with members of the dominant racioethnic group who are sincerely committed to introspection and the dismantling of systems of oppression. I (Tina) almost fell into this trap when Beth initially approached me, before Bridge could even begin: my general mistrust of White women led me to hold Beth at arm's length. Fortunately, I was able to dig, surface what was going on inside of me, and actively work to address the racialized trauma that contributed to my negative, interpersonal reaction to Beth despite Beth's consistent, positive efforts to connect with me.[11] Dig is a constant practice.

Employing a growth mindset

When you dig, you actively interrogate norms associated with a power-dominant group of which you are a member. You actively listen when people from historically marginalized backgrounds speak and do your best to set aside any defensiveness. With this frame, you are better able to listen, ponder new information that you may experience, and consider how you feel, think, and might behave in response to the new information. This growth mindset is the crux of Dig. Dig never ends; it evolves.

Fortunately, Dig provides the opportunity to continue to explore so that we can collectively work to dismantle systems of inequity. Dig is liberating in that it equips you to see the power structures and your place in this power structure at the individual, interpersonal, and institutional levels. This provides an opportunity to examine your multiple identities: those imbued with power and those that have been historically marginalized. It helps you surface your assumptions about these identities. Further, if you allow yourself to be curious, Dig will help you develop the skill of sitting in discomfort, interrogating your viewpoints, and building communities of authentic connection. In turn, those communities can forge ahead with collective action.

The ever-evolving nature of Dig can be either exhausting or empowering, depending upon your mindset. We live in a world of checklists and goal setting and accomplishment. But growth is an everlasting process. If you think of Dig as a goal to check off your personal checklist, it will limit your ability to truly interrogate yourself and thwart your ability to authentically bridge the divide that exists between you and women who are different from you. Shared Sisterhood as a process is the dynamic interplay between Dig on one hand and Bridge on the other, where authentic relational connections lead you to more self-discovery and empathy and risk-taking and vice versa. Assuming that the process marches in one direction will limit your growth. Never be afraid to come back to Dig.

Dig as a Path to Bridge

It can be challenging for White people to recognize that they, either as individuals or as members of a collective, have racially traumatized Black people, and members of other marginalized racioethnic groups, and that this trauma requires concerted individual, interpersonal, and systemic effort to overcome. Many members of power-dominant collective groups often want to proceed to Shared Sisterhood with historically marginalized group members without doing Dig. Time after time, we have observed dominant group members who want the benefits of Shared Sisterhood without self-interrogation and a commitment to redressing historical harms. Even those of us who have spent ample time doing Dig work, like Beth, can find ourselves in potential bridge situations with people who are not amenable to such connections because of the context in which we live.

When I (Beth) am acting authentically in line with my own values, I am expressive and open and enthusiastic. But my desire to connect cannot negate the fact that others may not desire the same. Authentic connections are exchanges that align with the true values, emotions, thoughts, and behaviors of each party—so my own authentic desires are not enough. I can invite; she can decline. I can hug; she can half-heartedly greet me in return. I must understand that this might be a temporary reaction that will change over time. Reading the signals that a connection is not truly authentic requires awareness of others, but also self-awareness via Dig. I have to use my Dig practice to examine my own actions but also to investigate the systems of power that surround the connection I am trying to make. I have to be sensitive to the personalities of others as well as to the context in which we are operating.

If I attempt to push such a connection when my partner is unwilling or not ready, I can compound the traumatic racist experiences that my partner has experienced in the past. I can think that I am the exception, but instead I may prove the rule—that White women will attempt to speed to Shared Sisterhood without demonstrating the trust, vulnerability, risk-taking, and empathy required to actually authentically connect. As human beings we have a fundamental need to connect and belong. However, connection attempts will likely be perceived as inauthentic and may be harmful if the initiator attempts connection while simultaneously ignoring the collective context that defines dominant and marginalized group membership. In other words, bridging without digging deeply enough will almost certainly backfire. Whether you are from a power-dominant or a historically marginalized group, Dig is designed to equip you with personal insights that help you successfully bridge.

When you dig, it is important that you understand yourself, and part of that understanding is assessing your readiness to bridge with others. While we will talk more about the interaction between Dig and Bridge in the next chapter, the role that Dig played in our Shared Sisterhood is very clear. Without Tina engaging in it at the outset of our relationship, we never would have been able to authentically connect. And without Beth engaging in it before we met, and throughout, we never would have been able to maintain our relationship.

Thinking, Feeling, and Doing

Think

Consider what you would think about yourself if you discovered that one of your social identities was associated with power in a way you did not know until you began to dig. How can you prepare yourself to manage the inevitability of defensiveness that often occurs when this happens?

Feel

What feelings do you have about the Dig practice? Are you nervous? Confident? Excited? Is there anything you fear you'll discover? What can those emotions tell you about your own Dig practice?

Do

Now that you have thought about potential reactions and considered your feelings as cues, write down a plan to help yourself check in with those emotions along the way. First write down the emotions you think you will most likely experience—fear, anger, excitement, shame, frustration, defensiveness, and so forth. Then write down what Dig steps you can engage in when you experience those emotions. This will help you be more prepared when you experience them in your Dig practice.

4

Bridging across Differences

W hile Dig is focused on the self, Bridge is focused on others. Bridging across differences means that women become Sisters by focusing on the creation of authentic connections facilitated by the perspective gained during Dig. A bridge is one connection between two points—or two people—and although that one bridge can get you part of the way toward equity and justice, Shared Sisterhood is predicated on the idea that one bridge will facilitate another and another, until there is a latticework of bridges connecting women and others who share the goal of equity.

What Is a Bridge?

A bridge occurs when people develop authentic connections across differences and those connections form the foundation for larger collective action toward equity. An *authentic connection* is when two people are able to express their internal experiences—their thoughts, beliefs, assumptions, ideas, and emotions—to each other and do so in a relationship characterized by trust, empathy, vulnerability, and risk-taking. While those four components do not have to be at the same level for both parties at all times, the goal is that both parties are willing to engage in such behaviors if needed or desired. Each time a pair of individuals connects authentically at work, they put down a layer of a bridge—and the more the two individuals authentically connect, the stronger the bridge between them becomes. Once a bridge is established between two initial individuals, each of them can then reach out to others to develop additional bridging relationships and connections.

A bridge is not the same thing as a friendship. A friendship is a relationship between two people who like each other, enjoy spending time and talking together, and are fond of each other, but a friendship does not necessarily entail addressing what you have learned during Dig: you can have an interracial friendship and never talk about racioethnicity or racism. In contrast, discussion about and consideration of racioethnicity and racism or any basis of systemic inequity is an essential component of the Bridge practice. Friendship may facilitate the Bridge practice and may be an outcome of the Bridge practice, but friendship is not a prerequisite for Bridge.

While friendship is not necessary to Bridge, value alignment is absolutely essential. Bridge connotes that both people are willing to pursue the dismantling of systemic inequities and address how those systemic inequities have permeated how they think about each other. Bridge is about trust, empathy, risk-taking, and vulnerability between two people so that they can link arms and pursue collective action based on their shared values. In that, Bridge partners become co-laborers in the pursuit of equity for all people, regardless of whether they would consider themselves true friends.[1]

Authentic, value-aligned connections

People connect in all sorts of ways every day—at work and elsewhere. We smile and nod at strangers out of politeness, we ask how our coworker's weekend was without really caring, we respond, "Fine, thanks, how are you?" when we are not fine. Much of this is part of our expected social contract, as politeness often prescribes such exchanges. And, in organizations, small talk (which is trivial, surface-level communication) can comprise up to a third of adult conversation.[2] Although this may be expected, and even necessary, for maintaining working relationships in organizations, in Shared Sisterhood we believe that *authentic connections* are necessary for sustained progress toward systemic equity (as shown in figure 4-1).

FIGURE 4-1

The necessity of authentic connections for sustained progress

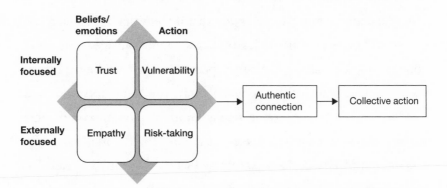

Source: Reprinted from *Organizational Dynamics: Special Issue on Power and Politics*, Tina Opie and Beth Livingston, "Shared Sisterhood: Harnessing Collective Power to Generate More Inclusive and Equitable Organizations," Copyright 2021, with permission from Elsevier.

Authentic connections are related to the "high-quality connections" (HQC) that have recently become part of the positive psychology movement. In the past twenty years, organizational scholars have moved from focusing on dissatisfaction at work, or turnover from bad jobs, to also recognizing the benefit of positivity and well-being at work. In work led by Jane Dutton, Emily Heaphy, John Paul Stevens, and colleagues, HQCs are focused on the "micro-bits of interrelating at work that can contribute to a relationship over time, but are important in and of themselves."[3]

Imagine you're at work and you're walking down the hallway with a colleague after a team meeting. Your colleague compliments the idea you shared moments before and you both pause for ten minutes, talking energetically about how you could execute your idea. Your colleague shares things you hadn't considered and is genuinely excited about the prospect of what you propose. As you say goodbye, you walk back to your desk with a pep in your step. This is what we would call a high-quality connection, characterized by an interaction between two people that is positive and energizing. Both you and your colleague expressed positive regard and trust, and you both were actively engaged as you interacted.

In contrast, imagine that instead your colleague approaches you after the team meeting and tells you that if you want to be taken seriously, next time you should learn to talk about your idea with more confidence—after all, no one will respect someone who doesn't respect themselves. As your colleague walks away, you feel empty and tired. This type of low-quality connection is common in organizational relationships and can leave employees feeling like their workplace is toxic and draining.[4] This drain is exacerbated when individuals already feel marginalized at work or in society.

There are important components of HQCs that are related to the authentic connections that compose the latticework of Bridge. High-quality connections have (a) "emotional carrying capacity," meaning the people interacting can handle sharing their true emotions with one another, (b) "tensility," where the interaction can hold up to strain or tension, and (c) "connectivity," where the interaction is open to new ideas and influences. Authentic connections in Shared Sisterhood also have these three components. But we add the idea of *"value alignment"*— the expectation of continued interactions into the future, such that our interactions are working toward a shared goal emanating from shared values, which may not be achieved until later. While HQCs may reflect microinteractions that occur in—or for—a moment, Bridge takes HQCs and focuses on how these connections can be built upon and maintained to serve a shared goal of equity. Bridge requires some expectation of continued interaction, at least until the goal is met, as building a foundation for collective action assumes a longer-term expectation of continuing to interact with someone else at work toward this goal. Critically, the HQC and value alignment is also not the endgame, as it may be with HQC; it is the mechanism for lasting collective action for equity.

Types of bridges

Bridges can be professional and personal and can be either short- or long-term in nature. In this book, we talk about Shared Sisterhood in the context of workplace equity, so we focus on professional bridges. A professional bridge is an authentic connection that occurs solely in a workplace context or that may occur outside of a workplace context, but for work-related purposes. This might be a connection where the relationship partners help each other learn how to master work tasks, navigate a workplace culture, or develop a network. The critical point is that these interactions are constrained to content that addresses professional aspects of life.

A personal bridge is an authentic connection that may occur inside or outside of a workplace context, but the content revolves around personal issues. This connection might be one where the relationship partners help each other overcome personal challenges such as the death of a loved one or celebrate shared interests such as movies, politics, television, and so forth. These interactions are constrained to content that addresses personal aspects of life.

Finally, some bridges are both professional and personal. This is the case with Tina and Beth. Over the years, we have discussed professional issues such as how best to analyze data, develop a research stream, publish in top-tier journals—and even how to write a book. Additionally, we have discussed personal issues such as parenting, marriage, politics, religion, and health. Importantly, so long as your connections are authentic, a bridge can be built whether it is professional, personal, or both.

Bridges can be short-term or long-term. Short-term professional bridges are typically characterized by situational challenges that can be addressed in a short period of time. This is similar to coalition building.[5] For instance, you may work on a project with a woman at work and connect with her authentically many times over the course of the project's eight-week duration, knowing that, once the project goals are achieved, you may never have reason to connect again. Although it is short-term in nature, the bridge is still worth pursuing to ensure that the project team is, and remains, as equitable as possible.

Bridges might also be longer in term, such as authentic connections that develop over an extended period of time. For example, like the bridge between Beth and Tina, it may be an indefinite long-term bridge, in which layers of authentic connection continue to build on each other, making the bridge stronger and more likely to withstand difficult future challenges as we work to improve equity within our workplaces (and society at large).

How Are Bridges Formed?

In order to provide concrete steps that you can take to create bridges with people who are different from you, we have to consider how bridges form. Because bridges consist of layers of authentic connections that occur over time, they often begin with an initial attempt to establish an authentic connection. In our Shared Sisterhood Clubhouse conversations, we have received back-channel messages that ask how to connect with someone ("Tina, where do I start?") and also attempt to connect ("Beth, I love what you said there—let's talk about this more!"). These differing outcomes emerge because the Bridge practice will often differ depending upon (a) the individual characteristics (things like personality, emotional intelligence, or prior bridge experience) and (b) power dynamics of those who are initiating the bridging and those who are receiving the bridge attempt.

The individual personalities of the people building the bridges affect how bridges form. People can vary in the degree to which they are assertive, social, modest, conflict-avoidant, and anxious—among other differences. There are myriad personality traits that may affect how one person interrelates with another. One woman, for instance, may enthusiastically and loudly engage with a colleague because that is her natural personality. That colleague may have a more anxious personality and hesitate or look away when responding, or not respond at all. These potential differences are always important to recognize when you are learning what it means to be authentic with a particular person. But these individual differences are not always separate from power dynamics. Stereotypes about personality traits are linked to many social identities. For instance, women in general may be stereotyped as warm and kind, so when they act more assertively, it can be unexpected.[6] Black women have been stereotyped as being angry, so when they act assertively, it can be used as confirmation of a stereotype.[7]

The wide gulfs that often separate Black and White women sometimes make even the creation of such bridges difficult. While Bridge is not the same thing as a friendship, the literature on interracial friendship is helpful to elucidate some of the challenges that different racioethnic bridge partners may confront. Unsurprisingly, racioethnicity is a barrier to friendships between White and Black women.[8] This is, at least in part, because of the unique history between White and Black women in the United States, given that White women benefited from and participated in enslavement, Jim Crow, and redlining, among other historical issues, while Black women were on the receiving end of such atrocities.

These historical patterns frame even how young people view interracial friendships. Kimberley Scott argues that the structure of de facto racial segregation in schools can lead young White girls to generally play the role of social leader, assuming that their Black female peers will follow, and because these young girls often do not have the Dig skills to understand the dynamics underpinning such assumptions, these Black/White interracial friendships can be hampered by White girls' lack of experience examining the broader structure of power in which they sit.[9] Giving young people the tools to dig and understand the history that affects racial connections, particularly in the United States, is key to the ability to bridge. If we want grown women who can authentically connect at work, we need to help young women and young girls understand how history informs the present so that they can bridge across racial differences.

Social science research on adult interracial friendships also supports our assertion that White women's historical understanding is a critical ingredient if adult women are to bridge across their racioethnic differences. When Granger studied Black and White women friends who had been good friends for at least five years, she found that the Black women respondents felt that meaningful dialogue—or friendship—had to be predicated on a common acknowledgment of racist history and structures that may affect their own interpersonal connection.[10] Research has found that White people tend to feel uncomfortable discussing racism.[11] This discomfort, however, pales in comparison to the trauma that can be reexperienced when Black women discuss the racism they have faced.[12] And yet, despite the trauma that Black women experience, they choose to engage in interracial conversations about racism because this common acknowledgment of shared values and understanding about racist history is critical to Bridge. Dig and Bridge are essential practices to help White people (and other power-dominant groups) work through their own discomfort and reticence to address how historical racism affects their relationships with Black people (and other historically marginalized groups) and to consider the importance of such recognition in their bridges.

For instance, when White people resist discussing racism with their Black friends, it can have negative relational effects. This is reflected in Granger's study as well, in which, sadly, one friendship was irreparably damaged by the study itself: when the friends were asked about racism, and the White friend considered it for the first time, their relationship never had the same level of closeness. Granger shares this story as a demonstration of the variance in interracial friendships among women—that some will ignore racioethnicity and others will confront it. Sometimes White women connect with who they *believe* their Black friends to be rather than who these Black women actually *are*, which precludes the authenticity that is needed for Bridge to succeed. The fact that, like the young girls in the study above, White women have not had to think about racioethnicity and identity in the same ways as their Black counterparts means that it is sometimes difficult to understand the collective experiences that people from historically marginalized groups often share. Unless and until White women are willing to surface and confront their own assumptions about racioethnicity, it will be difficult for them to bridge, and they might cause harm in their bridge attempts with Black women. This is why Dig and Bridge go hand in hand with constructing authentic connections that can withstand the dual forces of systemic racism and individual fear or inexperience.

In practice, bridging between people of different racioethnicities may be difficult if the relational parties are unable or unwilling to discuss racism. But this does not mean that every bridge interaction must be centered on racioethnicity or racism. Bridges are built brick by brick, conversation by conversation, interaction by interaction. Each brick does not have to be about racioethnicity. Once the bridge partners establish that they share similar values about dismantling inequity, they might need to develop trust by talking about other things besides racism, especially at the beginning of the Bridge process, when they are just getting to know each other. Establishing these shared values must be predicated on authenticity, however, as empty platitudes and virtue signaling in ways that are not reflective of partners' actual values will backfire, putting that particular bridge at risk of failure.[13] This is where Dig becomes so important. If you truly want to authentically connect, you must first get comfortable understanding your own discomforts around racioethnicity, gender, and other differences so that you can establish a bridge that reflects the other person's full humanity and achieve your shared equity goals.

Building Bridges across Racioethnic Differences

Like the centrality of racioethnicity in many interracial friendships, differences based on racioethnicity will often become relevant to the bridges that are built. Kiara Sanchez and colleagues characterize these different perceptions of experiences based on racioethnicity as "threatening opportunities" in that they can make the bridge stronger but can also threaten the bridge by challenging people's sense of themselves.[14] The competing emotions of fear and the desire to be understood are critical components of bridges across the span of differences, but, when recognized, they can serve to make authentic connections stronger and provide opportunities for learning. The nonparallel nature of bridge building and the centrality of racioethnicity to Shared Sisterhood means that we need to think particularly about what it means to build bridges from each direction—marginalized to dominant and dominant to marginalized—and our experiences can help provide some context to these considerations.

White women bridging with Black women

The aforementioned power dynamics underscore why Black women may have a collective distrust of White women. If you are a White woman attempting to bridge with a Black woman, we recommend that you never forget the importance of your Dig work. We discussed Dig as an ongoing practice and set of skills that can help you to understand your own identities and how your reactions may reflect different societal power structures and personal experiences. Initiating Bridge with women from historically marginalized groups requires recognition that your collective history (that is, your White history) may have caused pain for others. Thus, when White women attempt to bridge with Black women, for example, White women should understand that if Black women are aware of this history and if they have experienced workplace racism, they may find it difficult to trust White women or feel that demonstrating their authentic emotions or thoughts to a White woman at work is too much of a risk.

In our *Harvard Business Review* piece on the limits of inclusive climates, we found evidence that Black women were not alone in the perception that developing authentic connections with White women was risky. Our research revealed that when Black and Latinx/Hispanic women relied on other people to get their jobs done at work, they were less likely to feel comfortable sharing their authentic emotions with their coworkers, even if the organization boasted an inclusive climate. The risk was just too great. If the project failed, or the team's performance was subpar, the women from historically marginalized groups felt that they would shoulder a disproportionate amount of blame and could get thrown under the bus by their White colleagues, making them reluctant to build bridges with White people, even if the organization tried to make racial inclusivity a priority.

These fears are not unfounded. We know that people from marginalized racioethnic groups may be blamed more often for poor performance (like when minority CEOs are seen as more personally responsible for poor company performance) and people often misattribute blame and responsibility for mistakes and poor performance when the person making the mistake is different from them.[15]

As a White woman, I (Beth) know this, and I know that my own desires and even my own trustworthiness may be secondary to the experiences that my coworker has had with women who may have looked and acted just like me. If I want to build a bridge, I have to keep the four components of authentic connections in mind and work to establish trust via demonstrating my empathy, showing my vulnerability, and taking risks on her behalf. And above all else, I must center her concerns in my own Dig work, demonstrating empathy all while continuously educating myself.

If you're a White woman who is new to building bridges across racioethnic differences, this may seem like a lot to consider. And there may be some apprehension about how you will be received and how you might be judged if you make mistakes. I remember when I was younger, and I wondered why a group of young women I wanted to be friends with—predominantly Black women—seemed standoffish toward me. It hurt to not be included, when I was usually pretty well-liked, and I was acting in a way that I felt was engaging. I was listening, smiling, asking questions, and making eye contact. And yet, I felt like I was being pushed away. A mutual friend pulled me aside and said, "Don't worry. Once they realize you really care, that you're not like everyone else, they'll come around." And that comment stung. Because it meant that, as of that moment, they thought I *didn't* care. I was acting authentically. I was trying to be a good friend. And they were not interested in reciprocating.

I wanted to ask her what she meant, but because my personality is to avoid conflict and to be agreeable in all things, I smiled and nodded and left (though I realize some people's personalities would have led them to react in a very different way). Later, I thought about what she said about "everyone else," and it dawned on me that there were a lot of White women who may not have been interested in being a true friend. In fact, I knew plenty of White girls like this and had personally witnessed their harmful behaviors. While I did not recognize their behaviors as racist when they occurred, many of these White girls had said and done things that, upon reflection, were absolutely racist. The Black girls that I was trying to connect with surely had recognized these racist behaviors immediately, and I had not done or said anything to demonstrate that I was not the same. My ignorance and lack of action likely contributed to the Black girls' perceptions that I was not trustworthy.

Of course, I didn't see or understand any of this at the time—I only saw my own hurt at being left out. And it felt unfair that they would think that I was similar to those White girls who had been racist. Yet, I hadn't proved otherwise. Instead, I had hoped that my positive intent, and my good heart, would be clear to the Black girls, that they would see me as "Beth" and not as representative of a group that had caused harm. Later, I could see that their standoffishness toward me was a protective mechanism developed after earlier harm from White girls, and I had to take actions to warrant their acceptance, trust, and respect. And, even more importantly, I had to acknowledge that someone may not want to connect with me at that moment.

That individualistic perspective, where I focused on my own feelings and desires, more than those of others, is not uncommon. M. J. Collier's investigation of college friends suggested that communication patterns emerged among racioethnic groups, where Black Americans emphasized respect, while White Americans were focused on recognizing their own individual needs within the friendship.[16] Collier's further work on communication in friendships has suggested that White people may be more likely to see themselves as "unique individuals" as opposed to part of a group, a point of view that would make it more difficult to understand and connect with those for whom being part of a racioethnic group is a central part of their identity.[17] Racioethnicity is a social construct that allows me, as a White woman, the privilege of ignoring this identity when it suits me, but it does not afford everyone the same choice, since racial identities were foisted on people groups, complete with negative stereotypes and associations. So when I am trying to bridge with someone who is not White, I keep this in mind: sometimes it can't be about me and what I want, if my goal is to really connect with someone. I have to recognize that my group membership affects how others see me (and how I see others). Empathy is a critical element to help me pause to think about the situation from the perspective of the potential bridge partner.

If the bridge matters to you, you have to figure out how to pursue the bridge with someone who may be hesitant to bridge with you, recognizing that this may include discomfort and difficulty. Whether or not I want to admit it, I am connected to the collective trauma that White women have caused to Black women throughout history. What happened in the past may not be my fault, but what I do moving forward is still my responsibility, and I have to do the calculus as to whether sitting with my own discomfort was worth the connection. Now consider this example: When we were writing this book, Tina asked me, "What were you thinking when you were trying to bridge with me for the first time?" I realized that I did not think about it as bridge building at first. I was engaging with someone I thought was funny, smart, and kind— and who I thought would be a good friend and colleague. In our field, we do not always share an organization with our research colleagues, but our profession is small and insular, and we would see each other relatively often. Tina was always polite and friendly with me, but there was less authenticity in how we interacted at first. It felt very surface-level. Which, if I am honest, is what many of my professional relationships entail—polite, surface-level engagement. And usually, this is fine. But the more I got to know Tina, the more I wanted to build a bridge across the invisible gap that divided us. I just was not sure how to do that. So I began by telling her about myself and my interests, and

I asked her about her own. I demonstrated my shared values regarding racial equity in the words I spoke, but also in the actions I took. I attempted small authentic interaction after small authentic interaction, letting her reticence be a point of information for me to determine how I would go forward. I realized that, for this particular bridge, I needed to prove myself trustworthy—and even if I wasn't exactly sure why, I knew that it was worthwhile for me to persist.

Tina likes to say that it was my persistence that began to win her over, but it was surely also the fact that I was endorsed as trustworthy by a mutual friend—a Black woman. This endorsement provided Tina with additional evidence that our values were aligned regarding equity and she could talk to me about racioethnic inequity if she wanted to. As Tina and I exchanged authentic connections, our bridge began to build. Had I not met Tina's willingness to trust me with my own continued vulnerability and authenticity, it would have remained a rickety little crossbridge. But our continued sharing of our real and true emotions, our honesty, and our behavioral integrity built the bridge up stronger and sturdier. We started small and over time we shared more of ourselves, increasingly taking risks as we made ourselves more vulnerable to each other. Over time, our bridge became stronger and stronger, and we were able to delve even more deeply to understand each other and position ourselves to lead Shared Sisterhood in pursuit of collective action.

Black women bridging with White women

All four of the Shared Sisterhood components are important. Yet, as we can see from Beth's story of how she bridged with Tina, empathy emerged as a critical component, which may likely be the case for many White women. For Tina and many Black women, however, trust is often paramount.

As a Black woman, when I (Tina) think about bridging with White women, my primary concern is whether or not I can trust the person. As a result, I become hypervigilant for cues about someone's trustworthiness. Before, when I have jumped headfirst into relationships with White women, I have all too often been harmed. My prior experience has taught me that many (not all) White women colleagues may have a transactional approach with me in the workplace—competing with me and focusing on their own advancement, potentially at my expense.[18] In contrast, the vast majority of my prior experience has taught me that my Black women colleagues were more likely to have a relational approach with me, in which they were interested in both of us doing well and, overall, in the advancement of women and Black people.

Ella Bell and Stella Nkomo explain in *Our Separate Ways*, their book about how racioethnicity and class can serve as wedges between women, that my perception is not just my imagination, and that Black women may interact with each other differently than White women do.[19] In fact, Bell and Nkomo found evidence that Black and White women are often raised to have different approaches to people of their same race compared to those of different races. For example, the combination of common external forces such as White supremacy and the fact that there are often only one or a few Black women in a given organization, we are often raised to believe that success in the workplace is predicated on our ability to find one another to help each other learn how to survive and thrive in hostile workplace environments. Black women also often hear the message that they will have to work twice as hard to get half as far as their White counterparts. Hard work is assumed to be part of the journey.

Bell and Nkomo argue that White women are raised to do their best, to excel, to believe that if they work hard, they will ascend—and that it is solely up to them. While both Black and White women may be raised to assume that hard work is necessary, their perceptions on how they will succeed (via relationships versus on their own) and how they will be rewarded (perhaps less than what they deserve versus equally if they work hard enough) help to explain why Black and White women may have very different perceptions about the importance of connecting with other women in the workplace.

Beyond trustworthiness, value alignment is another way that I assess a potential bridge partner. As I contemplate bridging with a White woman, I also try to find out as much information as I can about her to determine if we share similar values about dismantling inequities. Has she demonstrated empathy, trust, risk-taking, or vulnerability with me or other Black women in the past? Has she spoken up publicly about systems, policies, and procedures that disadvantage Black women at work? Has she taken action to dismantle inequities?

After asking myself these questions and vigilantly scanning the environment for answers, I eventually decide whether or not to bridge with her. I could make at least two types of errors in this decision: I could say no, and later find out that the potential bridge partner was trustworthy, or I could say yes, and later find out that the potential bridge partner was untrustworthy. My caution when bridging with White women is based on the latter error. It has been devastating to me when I trust a White woman, attempt to bridge with her, and later discover that she did not have my best interests at heart, despite appearing to hold similar values. Unfortunately, this has happened numerous times throughout my career. It has largely been Black women, and Beth, who have helped me recover from these incidents.

My approach to Bridge may appear overly cautious or strict to some. But the individual-level trauma of anti-Black racism coupled with racist policies and procedures at the systemic level have manifested in my having a hard time trusting White people and institutions. This admission might startle some readers. You might wonder, "How can a person who is known as an expert in diversity, equity, and inclusion hold such emotions or thoughts toward others?" You might think that I should be more trusting, or perhaps that I am overreacting when I don such protective shells or act so cautiously. But I am human, and it is a natural human response to protect myself from individuals or groups of people who have traumatized people like me.

Perhaps another context can better elucidate this trauma. During the #MeToo movement, people—often women—shared the many steps that they take to avoid sexual assault or rape. For example, when getting into a cab, Uber, or Lyft, many women and victims of sexual assault are hypervigilant about their safety. They may take a picture of the driver and their license plate and text that information to a friend for safekeeping just in case something happens; they may dial 9-1 and have their finger positioned over the last 1 just in case they need help.[20] This hypervigilance—actively monitoring their surroundings—is often taught to people from historically marginalized gender groups to protect them so that they can stay safe and avoid trauma from men. This active monitoring is not based on a figment of their imagination, but because their personal experiences, the experiences of others like them, and history demonstrate that their safety may be at risk. These self-protective steps do not mean that the person hates all cab, Uber, or Lyft drivers, or all men: it means that prior trauma exacted by power-dominant group members (either their own or via the history of trauma targeted at people like them) has increased their awareness of the possibility of harm.

In contrast, many cisgender men may be surprised to learn that people from marginalized gender groups engage in such hypervigilance, because as a group, men are less likely to have had personal experiences and the group history to warrant hypervigilance to maintain their safety. This does not mean that men never experience danger; rather, it is less likely that men experience danger *because* of their gender. Similarly, we are not arguing that White people never experience hardship—just that it is less likely that White people experience hardship *because* of their racioethnicity.

In the same way, I am often concerned about trusting White women too quickly and often tread slowly as a protective mechanism. After all, it is unjust (and harmful) to ask historically marginalized people to stop using protective mechanisms when the systems against which they protect themselves still exist.

If I do decide that I am willing to trust a potential bridge partner, I begin the practice of Bridge. I try to find areas of overlap and explore how those common areas may bind us together. For example, perhaps the potential bridge partner is a fellow Christian. I might find out what Christian musical artists they like and, once I learn something that we hold in common, I emphasize that connection. I am establishing the bridge by first emphasizing commonality. Once we have formed a sturdy bridge based on commonality, I then begin to explore areas where we may differ, where we might have conflict, and where our respective organizations might benefit from collective action. In other words, I identify opportunities for action at both the interpersonal and systemic levels. I am testing the bridge. How open is the bridge partner to my thoughts about how we can connect? Are they willing to see my full humanity, or do they seem more comfortable when I adhere to racial stereotypes (for instance, by deferring to their leadership) or bristle when I use language like "Black women," "White women," "power," and so forth?

The Bridge practice occurs over time. The relationship that Beth and I have developed did not happen immediately. It has taken over a decade for us to create a strong bridge that is both personal and professional. Yet, it has been worth it. The fact that I know that I can trust Beth has helped me share my most authentic self and express my most vulnerable emotions and concerns. That trust has helped us build the book that you are reading. Together, we have written draft after draft, pouring our hearts into the book, and revealing who we are to each other in the process. The authentic connections that result from Bridge are worth the discomfort and pain that may come from forging those connections with people who have a different racioethnicity than you do.

Other examples of bridges

We have used our bridge as an example thus far, and although it's the most salient example for us, it is far from the only one. For instance, recall our earlier discussion of Chadwick Boseman and Sienna Miller. Boseman bridged with Miller on the movie *21 Bridges* across the span of racial and gender differences, authentically connecting through a series of interpersonal interactions characterized by trust, vulnerability, empathy, and risk-taking. Boseman shared his salary information and authentically connected with Miller because he empathized with her position as an inequitably paid actor. He did so under the expectation that their relationship would be ongoing, even after the current project ended.[21] Likewise, a solid bridge across the span of racial difference occurred when Jessica Chastain and Octavia Spencer authentically connected over pay inequity in Hollywood. Spencer took a risk and was vulnerable with Chastain, sharing her own experience with racism. Chastain listened, empathized, and engaged in authentic connection with Spencer to build an ongoing collaboration that resulted in explicit action: Spencer's salary was increased.

We also can see examples of Bridge with journalists Imani Gandy and Jessica Mason Pieklo, of Rewire News Group. Their public interactions on social media platforms like Twitter and on their popular podcast *Boom! Lawyered* demonstrates their deep connection, particularly focused on their shared legal and journalism backgrounds and their passion for reproductive justice. There's even a 2019 podcast episode that proclaims: "It's no secret that Rewire News legal eagles Imani Gandy and Jessica Mason Pieklo are as close as they are smart."[22] During the podcast episode, Gandy and Pieklo reveal particular experiences in their background that led them toward their work in social activism in reproductive justice, demonstrating how their individual Dig experiences led to their Bridge. They focus on their shared background and common interests and talk about what makes them different, and they discuss how these experiences have led them to where they are now, leading members of an organization built to conduct journalism and activism around reproductive justice.[23]

Our Shared Sisterhood Facebook group has sought to build more bridges across differences as well. We recall a recent example in which a public discussion occurred around the connections (and disconnections) between racism and anti-Semitism. A Black woman in our group wanted to understand anti-Semitism with more complexity and depth, and she publicly spoke out with her questions. She then organized a small group of Jewish and Black women on the thread to connect privately on this topic. They had cultivated their Dig tools and were desirous of an authentic connection so they could work toward a more equitable society and to better understand each other's experiences. These were women who had no prior connection except for their membership in our group, but they demonstrated their shared values and couched their questions in a recognition of their partners' full humanity. They worked to build their empathy and trust via demonstrations of vulnerability. We had created a culture based on the practice of Dig and Bridge in our Facebook group, which allowed our bridge to connect with and empower others to continue the process even without us being part of the conversation. This is what Shared Sisterhood can do—provide true opportunities for learning and growth and connection, while creating bridges that can be used to support collective action toward equity. When you educate people on the practices of Dig and Bridge, they are activated to independently pursue collective action and generate change throughout their lives.

Threats to Bridges

Bridges within Shared Sisterhood may face forces that crush and divide. That is one reason we describe Bridge as a practice that people *do*, not just something people build once and then forget about. Bridge partners must actively work to fortify their authentic connections so that these connections can withstand threatening forces. In turn, this series of connections among people can be conduits for change via collective action.

The negative forces and threats that may act upon Shared Sisterhood bridges can be either internal or external, in that there are forces internal to relationships between two people and forces external to them that can threaten these relationships.

Internal forces are often related to the power dynamics and structures we discussed above, and they can threaten the formation of the bridge by preventing authentic connections. Internal threats can include blind spots about racioethnicity or power that may lead to

inauthenticity in interactions or a refusal to continue being introspective about racioethnicity and power, and our own preconceptions via Dig. Because Dig is an iterative, ongoing practice, the refusal
to continue can make strengthening bridges difficult, leading to a
crumbling, weakened foundation. For example, we have seen White
women who felt that they were making inroads into a bridge with a
Black woman colleague. The White women pushed too quickly by
asking questions that did not demonstrate empathy. In turn, Black
women colleagues might respond with protective, less authentic
responses. Interactions characterized by such patterns may engender
mistrust in both people. With increased practice and expertise with
Dig, White women may become better able to recognize the need to
dig in these situations. Relatedly, as Black women get more experience with Dig, they may become more adept at recognizing why
they reacted less authentically and deciding if they would like to
communicate these reasons and eventually bridge.

It's important to note that sometimes threats to bridges can result
from acts of omission rather than commission. Bystanders who do
nothing in the face of racist, sexist, or other comments are not an
uncommon sight, and their inaction makes targets of such behaviors
feel worse. I (Beth) started working with the nonprofit organization
Hollaback in 2013, and I conducted a number of research studies in
conjunction with them. In a comprehensive study of experiences
shared by Hollaback! website contributors, we found that targets' negative experiences were exacerbated by the presence of bystanders who
did nothing when targets were harmed.[24] In a follow-up survey of
more than 16,600 people across twenty-two countries, we found
more evidence that reactions to harassment were more negative
when a bystander was present and did nothing than if there was no
bystander there at all.[25]

At the 1981 National Women's Studies Convention, the poet Audre Lorde spoke to the role of anger when allies—or bridge partners—do not speak up. She gave the keynote, saying that:

> I have seen situations where white women hear a racist remark, resent what has been said, become filled with fury, and remain silent because they are afraid. That unexpressed anger lies within them like an undetonated device, usually to be hurled at the first woman of color who talks about racism.
>
> But anger expressed and translated into action in the service of our vision and our future is a liberating and strengthening act of clarification, for it is in the painful process of this translation that we identify who are our allies with whom we have grave differences, and who are our genuine enemies.[26]

This quote demonstrates the interconnectedness of White women and Black women who have a shared value of equity, but it also illustrates how the collective trauma of racism can interfere with such a goal. When White women fail to act, become angry, and cannot (or do not) use Dig to understand whom they are really mad at, it can lead to cracks and divisions instead of stronger connections. As Audre Lorde notes, White women's unfurled anger can be misdirected at Black women who broach the topic of racism. But when those White women channel their anger toward taking action, taking risks, and demonstrating vulnerability and empathy, bridges via authentic connections are established and strengthened.

Directly addressing an observed racist act is a step toward fortifying your bridge with the target of the racist act. Luckily, workplace interventions in reaction to racist behavior are less likely to lead to violence than intervening during a case of street harassment—and they are also effective. In the book *Good Guys*, authors David Smith and W. Brad Johnson suggest that men step in when other men use sexist comments, calling out that sexism in the moment.[27] Likewise, we encourage people from historically power-dominant groups to immediately and directly step in when racist comments are made in their presence. Regardless of the intervention tactic, when you are facing threats from within your relationship—whether from your own (in)actions or because of your partner's—remember to place the focus on the person who has been or is being harmed. This will help you avoid damage to the bridges you have created.

A bridge must also withstand external forces that may threaten the relationship. A bridge must be able to weather the storm of institutional power structures that can make bridges difficult to establish in the first place or that threaten to destroy a bridge of authentic connection that has already been built. Such external threats may include colleagues or managers who make racist and sexist demands about the colleagues creating the bridge, a company whose incentives make authentic connections riskier, organizational cultures that allow little space or time for bridging to occur, or organizational processes that embed racioethnic or gender inequities but that are viewed as objective or normative. Even if both partners are connecting authentically and building a true bridge, other people who resent the bridge or have different goals may threaten it.

Research by India Johnson and Evava Pietri, for instance, finds that Black women may feel more trust toward their companies and belonging within them when they work at organizations that employ White women who are supportive of equity, and that White women can cue their trustworthiness and support by being endorsed by other Black women.[28] This research echoes the real-life story Beth told above about her initial bridging attempts with Tina: when White women build bridges, their bridges become signals for others, which can help build the latticework for collective action.

Bridges that crack and collapse

Sometimes the forces that act upon a bridge damage or destroy it. The bridge built between Belle Squire and Ida B. Wells-Barnett was likely challenged that 1913 day in DC at the Suffrage Parade. The external pressure from other White women to perpetuate the racial status quo surely strained it (as well as the many violent protesters on the sidelines). Was Wells-Barnett concerned that Squire and Brooks might capitulate, as she had likely experienced from White women many times before? It is hard to know for sure, but it is probable. However, the trio's desire to maintain the bridge likely provided a countervailing force for the three women, with every additional authentic emotional interaction bolstering the relationship they had built, solidifying it for the future. If Squire and Brooks had failed to act alongside and on behalf of Wells-Barnett, it would have increased the force of tension, exacerbating the ever-present stretching that may threaten bridges.

Bridges take time to build, and they are weaker when they develop cracks. Small cracks in a Shared Sisterhood bridge can lead to catastrophe if they are not identified and repaired. For instance, if your bridge partner moves too swiftly to deepen a connection, you might see it as a one-off warning, or it might signal a bridge-destroying breach in trust. Only the two relationship partners can ascertain the extent of the damage, as each connection is different. And the threats may not be the same for each set of Sisters. But the process for repair will always require the parties to return to Dig and build the bridge back up, starting with introspection about one's own role in the problem, and then repairing it, authentic emotional connection by authentic emotional connection.

Interpersonal bridge failures come at a great cost. Sometimes, small cracks are merely surface imperfections that can be resurfaced fairly easily. But other times, the crack may be irreparable and the bridge may collapse, requiring that it be redesigned and rebuilt. Trust must be rebuilt; empathy must be reestablished; relationships must be deemed solid by risk-taking and vulnerability. Yet, there is no certainty that the bridge will ever be the same again. In the exercise in the sidebar, "Repairing Bridges That Crack Together," we will work through how to handle challenges and cracks in bridges and talk about how the repair process differs based on who is responsible for the crack/damage and what the power structure acting as a force upon the bridge looks like.

Choosing to repair a cracked bridge

Our own experiences, and our interviews and surveys with historically marginalized women at work, indicate that the hypothetical scenario in the exercise in the sidebar is not an uncommon situation for women from historically marginalized groups. Perhaps this has even happened to you, where a White woman you thought was an ally remained silent when she observed a racist joke or made a comment about politics or the world that signaled that she has not done the Dig work needed for you to feel that you could trust her enough to build a bridge. How do you process that damage to the relationship?

If you decide that the bridge is worth saving, but your trust is shaken, you might consider setting boundaries around the repair,

Repairing Bridges That Crack Together: An Exercise

There are few worksheets and introspective exercises that can help develop bridging skills, particularly around repairing bridges that are damaged. In workshops that we run, we often work through a series of case studies to help build those specific skills. Below, we use the same approach to help you work on your bridging skills. We present a mini case that will allow you to practice your reflexive Dig and Bridge skills, while answering a series of questions to help you improve your ability to connect authentically with people who are different from you at work.

Think back to that 1913 women's suffrage parade in chapter 1. Belle Squire and Ida B. Wells-Barnett had built a bridge together by building the Alpha Suffrage Club in Chicago in early 1913.[a] The club was created to organize Black women in the face of White women working to ban all Black people from voting, and Squire was a vocal supporter of the effort to help Black women get the right to vote. And, when the systemic forces of racism threatened the bridge between Wells-Barnett and Squire, Squire and their friend Victoria Brooks engaged in risk-taking in front of other White women, and in an authentic, empathetic plea to Wells-Barnett, declared that they would walk with her, wherever she walked. They would not walk without her.

Now, think about the questions below, and consider the individual, interpersonal, and institutional factors that could influence your reactions.

1. If you were Wells-Barnett, how would you feel about Squire and Brooks's risky decision to walk with you?

2. If you were Wells-Barnett, what might you think would have led Squire and Brooks to take such a risk?

3. Bridges are characterized by authentic connections built on trust, vulnerability, risk-taking, and empathy. Which of these components were in action (or were missing) in the scenario?

Now, let's pretend that Brooks and Squire did *not* say anything in the backroom meeting with the Illinois delegation when Wells-Barnett was told to go to the back of the parade. Let's say that, instead, Squire waited until after the meeting, then privately said to Wells-Barnett, "It is wrong for them to treat you this way, and I am so sorry. I cannot wait until we can change this organization from the inside out!"

Given that Squire and Wells-Barnett had an existing bridge in the women's suffrage movement due to their creation of the Alpha Suffrage Club, let's answer some additional questions. Again, think about the levels as you consider the question.

1. If you were Wells-Barnett, how would you feel about Squire's private declaration of support?

2. In this scenario, if you were Squire, why might you have supported Wells-Barnett privately rather than publicly?

3. Bridges are characterized by authentic connections built on trust, vulnerability, risk-taking, and empathy. Which of these components were in action (or were missing) in the scenario?

This exercise allows you to think about threats to a bridge, and bridge repair, within Shared Sisterhood in an important way. Understanding what the parties are thinking, feeling, and doing is a critical first step. The second step—identifying the varying influences on these thoughts, feelings, and actions—is equally important. This is not to diffuse blame or excuse behavior—it is to understand reasons. Excuses for actions are not the same as reasons for them. The Dig process requires us to ask these questions and to understand ourselves better, and the Bridge practice expands this questioning and understanding to a relationship between two specific people, which can require us to become well practiced in moving between digging foundations and building bridges and repairing those bridges when they are damaged (by ourselves or with others).

Notice how both feelings and actions can be influenced by multiple levels—individual personalities and histories, interpersonal relationships and interactions, and systemic pressures and harms. Also notice that each party in this scenario may have their own views about the scenario and its implications. We've talked about understanding our *own* reactions to and experiences with racioethnicity. But when enacting Shared Sisterhood, you also have to use your empathy to try to understand the person you're bridging with. To do this effectively, you need to have experience with the Dig process, trying to understand yourself and your proximity to power systems across your various identities, as well as your position in those systems. Otherwise, your empathy and perspective-taking may be clouded by your biases. For example, it is possible that if Squire had failed to publicly support

Wells-Barnett, Squire would not see her actions as damaging to her bridge with Wells-Barnett. In fact, she may see her actions as empathetic and supportive. After all, Squire acknowledged that the White women organizers had poorly treated Wells-Barnett, and Squire had put plans in place for actual structural change later. Even if Squire and Wells-Barnett had a history of trust and action, Squire may be blind to how Wells-Barnett may feel unsupported in that interaction. This blindness is a challenge to the bridge itself. In fact, had Squire heard the racist remarks, saw Wells-Barnett's emotion, and said nothing in the moment, instead choosing to express her support privately, Wells-Barnett may have felt betrayed, hurt, or angry because Squire did not take a public risk on Wells-Barnett's behalf.

a. A copy of the March 18, 1914, Alpha Suffrage Record is available here: http://livinghistoryofillinois.com/pdf_files/The Alpha Suffrage Record, Volume 1, Number 1, March 18, 1914.pdf.

using your own Dig process and the components of authentic emotional interactions, for instance:

- Taking a break from the interaction and asking for empathy/understanding (demonstrates vulnerability, encourages empathy)

- Sharing your authentic emotional reactions to the breach of trust/damaging situation (demonstrates vulnerability, invites trust)

- Establishing touchpoints that would indicate progress toward repair (demonstrating where a relationship partner or colleague could demonstrate risk-taking or vulnerability to inspire increased trust)

Tactics like this could help rebuild a bridge that was damaged due to a situation like the above, and they could allow the partner from the historically marginalized group who was targeted by the statement or situation to reestablish boundaries and set the terms for the trust repair.

Apologies as repair work

Alternatively, perhaps you're a White woman who witnessed a colleague direct a racist comment at a colleague from a historically marginalized group. Did you speak up at that moment? Did you redirect the conversation or push back against the problematic assertion? Critically, was there a member of that marginalized group present at the time? Did you center the experiences and emotions of the marginalized person or focus on your own? Or did you perhaps freeze in the moment and only after the fact think to approach that person to provide your support or concern?

Now, envision that the person targeted by that comment, or most negatively affected by it, is someone you consider a Sister. Or even a colleague that you hope to bridge with in the future. Did you pause to think about the situation from their perspective? Items adapted from the Interpersonal Reactivity Index can help us empathize as we bridge:

1. Have I tried to understand my colleague better by imagining how things looked from their perspective?

2. Have I looked at all sides of the question/situation?

3. Have I imagined how I would feel if I were in my colleague's place?[29]

We can practice asking ourselves these questions; using the answers to inform ourselves of (a) when we need to dig more and (b) when we need to bridge more can help make us less likely to freeze up, reducing the risk of damaging a bridge or precluding it from emerging in the first place. Such reflexive engagement in Dig and Bridge can strengthen relationships via authenticity, setting the stage for future collective action.

If you have failed to speak up in the presence of racism, apologizing is a critical component for moving forward. But there are ways to apologize that facilitate Shared Sisterhood, and there are ways that do not. Specifically, apologies are best received when they demonstrate accountability and sincerity. In her *Medium* article on "The Violence of White Apologies," author Ciarra Jones says it well: "What many white people fail to understand is that when an apology is devoid of accountability, it is doubly harmful to Black people."[30] It is difficult to accept an apology from someone who doesn't seem to own their responsibility for the offense. Sincerity is another critical aspect of apologies: when apologizing, it is also essential to sincerely acknowledge the harm that you have caused. Placing yourself, your feelings, and your position of power at the center makes apologies insincere and displays a lack of accountability— and each inauthentic connection damages the bridge further. Anecdotally, forgiveness in the wake of racist statements is more likely to occur when the perpetrator takes responsibility for their actions.[31] Additionally, a 2005 research study examined how sincerity and accountability affected reactions to apologies.[32] People were more likely to forgive a perpetrator when the perpetrator sincerely apologized, accepting responsibility for their behavior, and worked to fix the harm that they had caused. Apologies are best received when they accompany deep Dig work and are in service of repairing a breach that you take responsibility for. So, when you apologize, keep these tips in mind:

1. Have I done the work to determine why I engaged in the behavior I'm apologizing for?

2. Have I placed my Sister at the center in this apology, empathizing with her and taking her perspective on the situation?

3. Have I decentered my emotions and my feelings? In other words, if you cannot apologize without crying or centering your own feelings, please continue to dig until you can.

4. Have I paired my apologetic words with apologetic action? Accountability and sincerity mean making it right. Identify actionable ways that you will repair what went wrong and/or prevent it from happening again.

Bridges toward Collective Action

While authentic connections are the critical building blocks of Shared Sisterhood, these connections are not the end goal. These connections form the foundation of bridges, and as these bridges grow stronger, we can invite others to join as well, creating a lattice-work of bridges. Bridges across differences are catalysts for organizational and societal racial and gender equity via collective action that is the goal of the Shared Sisterhood philosophy.

The importance of bridges to collective action, and the lasting ramifications of not having bridges, is evident in our story of Ida B. Wells-Barnett and the Suffrage Parade. Wells-Barnett, Squire, and Brooks managed to connect across racioethnic differences in a time when it was socially frowned upon (and potentially illegal) for White and Black women to interact in the ways that the trio did. Yet, they built a bridge through a series of connections over time, because of their shared interest in women's suffrage. Indeed, throughout history, Black and White women have attempted collective action on such issues as suffrage, abolition, reproductive rights, education, gender roles, and workplace equity with varying levels of success. Regarding suffrage, there was positive momentum for interracial collective action when the Women's Loyal League, founded by Eliza-beth Cady Stanton and Susan B. Anthony, was created to end the Civil War by abolishing slavery. This was no small feat. According to Angela Davis, a world-renowned activist and scholar, Angelina Grimké's speech at the League demanded "civil and political rights of all citizens of African descent and all women," demonstrating an understanding of how racioethnicity and gender equity are intertwined.[33]

Yet, the suffrage movement took a turn for the worse when White women prioritized gender over racioethnicity. The plight of Black people, Black women in particular, was sacrificed so that White women could advance. The bridge that Wells-Barnett, Squire, and Brooks had built meant that they did not fall into this trap. The trio would surely have been aware of the racist political motives that drove many White suffragettes to exclude Black women from the suffrage movement, but this did not prevent them from continuing their interracial efforts to secure the franchise. We believe that the trio was able to persist because they successfully bridged.

The fact that other White women did fall into this "us versus them" trap suggests that they may have failed to bridge with Black women. A bridge would have meant that White suffragettes had developed authentic connections with Black women such that the White women viewed the Black women as having a common fate, value, and importance. Instead, the White women engaged in a zero-sum game in which gender was prioritized over racioethnicity. In her book *The Woman's Hour: The Great Fight to Win the Vote*, Elaine Weiss notes that White suffragettes argued that because White women outnumbered Black women, White supremacy would not be threatened by women's suffrage, in an attempt to influence White male legislators to pass legislation that would allow White women to vote.[34] Eventually, this racist influence tactic worked, and in 1920 the Nineteenth Amendment was passed, granting White women, in law and in practice, the right to vote.

It is possible that the White suffragettes did not intend to ignore Black women's concerns. But regardless of their intent, the fact that so many White suffragettes did not have bridges with Black women meant that the impact of their behavior ignored the rights of all women as a collective, instead elevating the voting rights of White women alone. This failure of collective action reverberates through the present-day women's movement. Despite the fact that Black men were legally allowed to vote, the great majority of Black people, including Black women, were disenfranchised until the passage of the Voting Rights Act of 1965. This lost time caused irreparable damage in racioethnic equity and in the collective trust between Black and White women. White women's push for gender equality and feminism was not strong enough to motivate White women to act on behalf of Black women after White women advanced toward greater equity with White men: White women sacrificed Black women at the altar of White women's enfranchisement. Such racist decisions are not easily forgotten and often permeate current interracial relationships between women, especially Black and White women, as demonstrated in much of the research we reviewed in this chapter. Without Bridge—and the Dig that could have facilitated such connections—collective action toward equity was difficult to achieve.

The journey of Shared Sisterhood reflects the movement from Dig to Bridge to collective action in order to achieve racioethnic and gender equity at work. Bridges between people at work are positive in and of themselves, and increasing the number of these authentic connections characterized by trust, vulnerability, empathy, and risk-taking is a good thing. But it is their ability to serve as the foundation for change that we highlight here. In chapter 5, we talk more about what it means to act as an interracial collective toward racial and gender equity and how Dig and Bridge affect change.

Thinking, Feeling, and Doing

Think

Think about a relationship you have with someone who holds different identities from you. What introspective work had to be done to build a sturdy bridge with this person? What did you discover about yourself, and how could it affect your authentic connection?

Feel

Can you think of a time when you didn't speak up in defense of a colleague or friend in a moment where they were treated poorly at work or elsewhere? How did you feel? What emotions were present? How did you feel—and how do you expect they felt?

Do

We talked about apologetic actions and taking accountability for your actions and words (or lack thereof) as ways to repair a bridge. Make a list of the words you could use to apologize for not speaking up, and the actions you could take to do so. Share this list with a trusted Sister, friend, or colleague.

5

Collective Action

I da B. Wells-Barnett and Belle Squire may have appreciated their authentic, deep relationship for the individual and interpersonal rewards it brought them; what made it true Shared Sisterhood was how it created the opportunity for lasting collective action for women's suffrage. With Shared Sisterhood, we radically reimagine power to facilitate action toward a goal of gender and racioethnic equity at work. We envision a system where authentic connection is created via the one-to-one connections between people at work, which builds into connections with others, providing a powerful latticework to pull everyone up together. Shared Sisterhood is a critical tool for creating systemic change via what we call *collective action*—when historically marginalized and dominant group members work together toward the same equity goals.

We noted at the end of chapter 4 that bridges serve as a conduit for collective action. Each authentic connection begets the opportunity for additional connections, until you have generated a latticework of connections that are primed to dismantle systemic inequities (as

FIGURE 5-1

The power of building bridges, growing connections, and creating collective action

This figure demonstrates how one bridge between Sisters can develop into a latticework of authentic connections that can lead to collective action. As two people solidify their bridge, they can bring their other connections into the collective through continued opportunities for authentic connection and the power of vouching for others' trustworthiness when dealing with issues of equity.

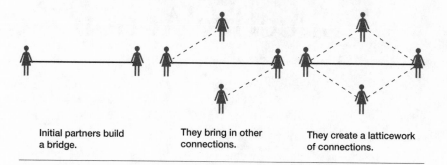

Initial partners build a bridge.

They bring in other connections.

They create a latticework of connections.

depicted in figure 5-1). Specifically, when a critical mass of people have bridged together, they can exert pressure and power within their organization via collective action. This means that no one person will be responsible for the movement, but rather the group of Sisters coordinates efforts, determining who is best positioned to say what, when, and to whom, always circling back to the group as more information is obtained, more power amassed, more goals accomplished. This pursuit toward equity in the form of collective action is the goal of Shared Sisterhood.

What Is Collective Action?

Collective action is a term with a long academic history. Traditional economic theory has often held that people may be unlikely to help others because rational actors will consider their own self-interest above all else.[1] This assumption, however, is often wrong.[2] Instead, people will cooperate—and act collectively—because they care about other people and desire both connection and belonging.[3] This persistent expectation that people *will* act individually in their own self-interest, and that they *should* act in such a way, means that the natural desire to connect and work together is seen by many as irrational and overly emotional. We argue that this is a very myopic, though all too common, view of human behavior. In fact, we argue that people working together, building relationships, and connecting authentically act as a critical driver of change by radically reimagining what it means to be in someone's "collective best interest." In Shared Sisterhood, collective action is not just about "what's good for me," but "what's good for us." Importantly, this collective action is driven not merely because of a self-interested desire to get ahead, but because the values of collective action toward equity are shared by Sisters, forming the motivation behind our desires to bridge with others who are different than we are and providing a foundation for efforts to change outcome and cultures toward equity.

While traditionally collective action was seen as transactional and individualistic, merely a mechanism through which individuals can achieve outcomes that benefit themselves alone, Shared Sisterhood suggests a more transformational view of collective action toward equity. When built upon the foundation of bridges built across differences, it can truly be about "we" instead of "me."[4]

The effect of difference on collective action

The Shared Sisterhood framework requires both historically marginalized group members and power-dominant group members to interrogate their identities and to mobilize together. But just as we discussed in Dig and in Bridge, there are differences in the ways that people may interact with the collective as it works toward equitable solutions. Collective action is an effective tool for addressing social inequity—but because it centers on historically marginalized people, it often gets less attention in psychological research.[5] Right now, research suggests that change will come from either reducing prejudice of dominant group members, for example, by engaging in Dig *or* by mobilizing collective action among people from marginalized groups, like women's marches that consist only of women.

Because these two approaches can have conflicting effects that may end up preserving the status quo power structure, the Shared Sisterhood philosophy combines them. While research suggests that when people share a collective identity, prejudice can be reduced, this collective identity could fail to challenge the ways in which power in society actually is wielded. It also does not acknowledge that people in disadvantaged groups often want to preserve their own identities without being subsumed into a broader identity, particularly when that identity fails to challenge inequitable power systems.[6] And while prejudice reduction focuses on social cohesion and reduced conflict, it does not provide a framework for building lasting, authentic relationships. As Stephen Wright and Micah Lubensky put it, "However well-intentioned they may be, many procedures used to reduce prejudice (e.g., intergroup contact) may also serve to undermine collective action by the disadvantaged group."[7]

In order to work together toward equity, people in the collective must perceive that there is a discrimination problem to be solved. It becomes more difficult to mobilize when this discrimination is more subtle and less obvious.[8] Therefore, increasing the awareness of current inequity and mobilizing the group with collective anger at injustice is a critical step in moving people toward change. Such mobilization follows something called the "social identity model of collective action," where a perceived injustice shared among the group can be a critical motivator of action.[9]

Having all people in a collective understand the historical injustices that have affected marginalized racioethnic groups is thus a critical component of collective action, which is facilitated via Dig and Bridge. Dig increases awareness of the existing power systems and one's own racioethnicity and biases, and Bridge leads to authentic connections that encourage shared indignation and/or a willingness to believe and listen to historically marginalized bridge partners and collectively act to solve problems of inequity. For collective action to result, the partner from the dominant group must communicate their understanding of the injustice and indicate their agreement that action is needed via their many authentic interactions with their partner.[10] (See the sidebar "Trust: A Critical Mechanism toward Action.") When sisters dig into their preconceptions about racioethnicity and agree on the problem of inequity, it is an important foundation for future action.

Not just allyship

Dig, on its own, is valuable, as self-knowledge and awareness have value. Bridge, on its own, is valuable, as true, authentic human connection has value. Shared Sisterhood combines these two practices to build a foundation to pursue true, long-lasting collective action. Too often, ostensible allies sacrifice the relationships and connections they have in the quest of power (in the name of equity). We saw it in the 1913 Suffrage Parade when Grace Trout, the White woman leader of the Illinois contingent, decided to capitulate to the racism of the Southern members

Trust: A Critical Mechanism toward Action

Even in the eighteenth century, Hume wrote about a "common sense of interest" that produces mutual expectations of behavior toward a common goal. This common interest leads to increased trust, which allows people to work together.[a] He argued that people generally understand the benefits of cooperation; they just need to learn to extend that trust beyond their nearest social circle—like via Dig and Bridge with Shared Sisterhood.

This trust can also emerge in organizations in ways that promote collective action. The "arithmetic of trust" between individuals takes into consideration the history between two people who know each other already. However, when colleagues do not have such a history, they have less information to work with to decide whether to take the risk to trust someone they don't know well. An

of the march—she was Wells-Barnett's ally, until she faced consequences for it. These utilitarian coalitions are often too weak to be the foundation for lasting change. When we focus on whether members of dominant groups perceive themselves as allies, we center the status quo of power—we assume that change is dependent upon members of the dominant group alone. Shared Sisterhood is different because it encourages collective action where power-dominant and historically marginalized people are working side by side.

There are a few different kinds of supporters to keep in mind as we pursue collective action—and not all of them are very effective. Thus far, we have used the term *ally* to describe members of domi-

overarching identity—like "Apple employee" or "professor"—can help overcome a lack of history by making colleagues feel like they're part of the same team and reducing the perceived risk of trusting someone.[b] Shared Sisterhood takes the idea of overarching identity and builds upon it by explaining how to overcome mistrust that is a result of historic racism, xenophobia, or other systemic discrimination that has divided people by demographics. Shared Sisterhood focuses a group on a shared goal of equity that uplifts everyone in a nontransactional manner. Each authentic bridge that is built between members in the collective makes the effort stronger and more likely to succeed.

a. You can see a discussion of Hume's work here: https://ipg.vt.edu/content/ipg_vt_edu/en/DirectorsCorner/re--reflections-and-explorations/Reflections092118.html.

b. Roderick M. Kramer, Marilynn B. Brewer, and Benjamin A. Hanna, "Collective Trust and Collective Action," *Trust in Organizations: Frontiers of Theory and Research* (1996): 357-389.

nant groups who want to aid members of historically marginalized groups. Allyship may be insufficient to dismantle systems of inequity. Dr. Tiffany Jana, a DEI consultant and public speaker, notes that an ally is someone who believes in equity in theory. Allies may read trending anti-racism books, discuss what they read in book clubs, and even post key learnings on their social media.[11] In Jana's conceptualization, this is typically the extent of allyship; they do not tend to develop deep relationships with members of historically marginalized groups.[12] Even research suggests that allyship can center power-dominant (that is, White) people rather than members of historically marginalized group members.[13] Recently, research has acknowledged this fact and resulted in more Afro-Diasporic definitions of allyship (Samantha Erskine and Diana Bilimoria provide a definition that is helpful and aspirational, for instance).[14]

Then there are accomplices, who, according to Jana, are individuals who work to actively dismantle systems of inequity, but not necessarily with the input of members of historically marginalized groups. They react to inequity and are willing to use their privilege to pursue equity, but without the bridges that we recommend with Shared Sisterhood.

Finally, there are *co-conspirators*, a term first coined by Ella Bell and Stella Nkomo.[15] Jana describes these individuals as those who work side by side with members of historically marginalized groups to proactively understand how best to dismantle systems of inequity. Co-conspirators respect that members of historically marginalized groups may already be engaged in efforts toward equity, and rather than co-opting these efforts, co-conspirators submit to the leadership of the historically marginalized communities. Co-conspirators use their advantage on behalf of others, recognizing that they may be best suited to overcome some challenges.

Using this categorization, Bridge is the joining of two co-conspirators, which centers the interests and concerns of the historically marginalized group member. Because of a shared goal of equity, power-dominant people then take risks and experience discomfort in the interest of eliminating inequities to benefit historically marginalized community members. When Bridge moves toward collective action, Shared Sisterhood prioritizes the authenticity of the connection and the goal of reducing inequity over individual comfort or goals. In other words, a historically dominant group member feeling good about being an ally is not what Shared Sisterhood is all about.

Take our relationship as an example. We lived Shared Sisterhood before we began to write about it. Our bridge—the connection that spans the gap between our personal experiences—is characterized by sharing vulnerabilities, establishing trust, demonstrating empathy, and taking risks. To establish, and maintain, our authentic connection, we had to engage in Dig on our own, both before we met and continuously. Then, our bridge became the tool through which we were able to make change in our own lives and communities. We brought our other connections into our bridge, working on efforts toward improving racial and gender equity in our profession of academia—and to bring this book to you. But, importantly, our goal was always about improving equity, and even when we had to address issues that brought us personal discomfort, we returned to Dig and to authentic connection to keep us moving in the direction of systemic change.

Collective Action at Work

Collective action toward equity can include one member of a bridge of Sisters pursuing equity, informed by their authentic connection. They may not always be working together: sometimes one person is pulling another up with them. It can also include both partners working side by side as a united front: together, they partner and work toward change. Collective action can also include more than two partners, in a larger collective, who all do what they can where they can to move their organization or group toward fairer, more just practices and outcomes.

Showing what we mean by collective action toward equity is critical. If Shared Sisterhood can help us achieve actual goals of racioethnic and gender equity in workplaces and jobs all around the world, what does that look like? We can learn from other efforts toward collective action how the principles of Shared Sisterhood can help move us toward equity, whether in Hollywood, academia, the tech industry, or beyond.

Taking on Hollywood: Ava DuVernay and Queen Sugar

Ava DuVernay has had a tremendous positive influence in the television and film industry, as well as in society at large. From her 2012 Sundance Film Festival award (the first ever awarded to a Black woman director) to her Golden Globe and Oscar and Emmy nominations, DuVernay has prioritized presenting the fully realized lives of Black and other underrepresented minority characters in her movies and shows.[16] In her work DuVernay has focused on events of critical importance to civil rights efforts, including *Selma, 13th,* and *When They See Us.* Additionally, her efforts on the drama *Queen Sugar* represent a true application of the Shared Sisterhood framework.

In 2015–2016, women directed only 17 percent of American television shows, with only 3 percent directed by women from historically marginalized groups.[17] Women often faced exhortations to "get more experience" in order to direct and write in Hollywood, but few gave them the opportunities to do so. So, when Ava DuVernay started production on *Queen Sugar,* she entered the game as one of a very few directors who were women of color at the time.

DuVernay was not content to just be one of the few who "made it," however, and she soon made it clear that she was going to uplift other women around her by hiring only women directors, focusing particularly on Black and other women of color to direct episodes for *Queen Sugar.* The effect was swift. Soon, the writers' room was majority female, and most key positions were helmed by women as well.[18] DuVernay took a risk by investing in others, creating systems that provided less experienced people with opportunities. But it was not just the systemic risk-taking on behalf of others with less power and opportunity; it also included interpersonal empathy and vulnerability. The producing director of *Queen Sugar*, taking her example from DuVernay herself, empathizes with the insecurities and uncertainties of being new to directing and reassures new members of the *Queen Sugar* team.[19] They even consciously fight against the common competitive norms that often pit women against each other. An interview in the *Lily* quoted producing director DeMane Davis: "A lot of the times, we're in this situation where there aren't that many women. And I'm Black, so there are definitely not that many Black women. So, when another woman comes up, it might be like, 'They only let one in. It's going to be me or you.' But [on *Queen Sugar*], it's not like that. It's all women. They're letting all the women in." This systemic change leads to women feeling interpersonally safe to enact the philosophy of Shared Sisterhood to uplift everyone in the organization.

DuVernay herself got her opportunity in television from two trailblazing Black women. Acclaimed showrunner Shonda Rhimes gave DuVernay her first opportunity to direct in television, inviting DuVernay to lead an episode of *Grey's Anatomy*. Then, Oprah Winfrey provided DuVernay with a platform (via Winfrey's Oprah Winfrey Network) to launch her own show, *Queen Sugar*, which Winfrey executive produces. DuVernay now provides those same opportunities to other women, creating systems within her companies that drive collective action.

Will DuVernay's efforts lead to sustained change in gender and racioethnic equity in Hollywood? Other institutions in television are seeking to make change in line with her efforts. Lifetime initially partnered with the American Film Institute to provide women with opportunities to direct on the show *UnREAL*, in conjunction with another female showrunner, Sarah Gertrude Shapiro, which resulted in greater representation of women directors.[20] Partnerships such as this are important, and they also represent the benefits of building relationships—Shapiro was a graduate of the same program she partnered with to provide experience for other women, showing how interpersonal connections can lead to institutional action.

Susanne Bier, another woman television director, has argued that television allows and accepts more risk than other components of Hollywood and argued that film needs to "catch up."[21] Other components of Hollywood can certainly learn from DuVernay's lead and incentivize risk-taking and empathy to provide opportunities for others who have not historically had them. Lasting change cannot be dependent upon one woman's investment in Shared Sisterhood. But it's an excellent place to start.

Fighting organizational discrimination:
Timnit Gebru and Margaret Mitchell

In 2020 and 2021, Google fired Timnit Gebru and Margaret Mitchell, two women who led Google's Ethical AI team. Google's decision to fire them was covered in the press as people alleged that the two were fired because they had highlighted racioethnic and gender inequities at Google. We have followed these two women's story for a number of years as the public has had a unique vantage point into their struggles for equity. And within the articles and interactions we observed, we can see a rich example of Shared Sisterhood. Their story is one that demonstrates how bridges can serve as a mechanism to work toward equity within teams, organizations, and across industries, even if Gebru and Mitchell did not accomplish their ultimate equity goals within the bounds of their own organization.

Mitchell and Gebru developed their interests and expertise in fairness and ethics in artificial intelligence separately, but their paths converged. When Mitchell, who had joined Google a few years earlier, became aware of Gebru's research on bias in AI, she asked Gebru to join her team focused on ethical AI. But Gebru recognized the risk of joining a company that was not diverse in terms of racioethnicity or gender; she knew it would be an uphill battle toward equity, and friends had warned her that the environment might prove hostile to her as a woman of color.[22] But Mitchell encouraged her—she had hopes that, if they stuck together, they could make real change.[23]

Soon after, however, they started to see racist and sexist patterns in the organization that confirmed Gebru's concerns. The duo had hoped they could combat it from within. Instead, they reported feeling isolated as they continued to attempt to move the organization toward equity. *Wired* reports that in 2019 Gebru and Mitchell created an internal document to bring these gender inequities to light. When they had a meeting with higher-level managers to talk about their own experiences with inequity, they did so together, side by side. Sometimes this bridge worked—pointing out their inequitable experiences together during this meeting resulted in Gebru being rightfully promoted when she had been initially hired at a lower level, and Mitchell was finally able to switch away from a supervisor whom she felt had treated her unfairly. But their work to use their bridge as a conduit for collective action within Google would result in backlash and, ultimately, both of them were fired.

When they were fired—Gebru in late 2020, and Mitchell soon thereafter—we learned about how the bridge between them served to work toward equity. In many articles about their ouster they were described as a "professional and emotional tag team, building up their group," and they bonded over "a shared desire to call out injustices in society and the tech industry." Mitchell said, "We got along on every dimension."[24] Together, they wanted to change their organization from the inside, and they had hoped that they could "share the burden and the limelight in hopes that together they could nudge Google in a more conscientious direction."[25] They worked together to do this, and based on their reports of their time at Google and their social media posts, they made a number of sacrifices together to fight the sexism and racism that they faced while they were there to make their immediate work team a more equitable environment. In that, their Shared Sisterhood was apparent—within their team, their bridge led to collective action toward equity.

Mitchell and Gebru used their individual bridge that they had cultivated to build bridges with others so that they could collectively work toward positive outcomes within their work group and their company. Their group was by all accounts a light of equity in their organization. They took pride in the diversity of their team, and *Wired* reported that Gebru saw that diversity as a critical asset to the team. Their team reached out individually to people within the firm to push them to think more ethically and equitably.

Their efforts beyond their immediate work group were met with opposition and, after Gebru was fired, allegedly for calling out what she described as unequal treatment, Mitchell took a risk, continuing to build on their bridge even after Gebru was let go. Mitchell publicly called out the trauma that Gebru's racist and sexist treatment caused their team, given that they were all closely linked.[26] *Wired* reported that Mitchell built an automated script to search her corporate email account for notes to help support Gebru and document the racism and sexism that they had faced together. Google fired Mitchell soon thereafter.

We continue to see the ways in which the duo's bridge has been maintained, even if only via public interactions. On Twitter, you can continue to see how Gebru and Mitchell's interactions and connections continue, for instance, when they characterized how they navigated discrimination at Google by standing up for one another and fighting their treatment together.[27] Their bridges within their group also affected lasting change. Their manager quit, at least in part because of how his employees were treated. Some academics backed away from the company in solidarity. And as Gebru launched a new organization, Distributed Artificial Intelligence Research Institute (DAIR), she has continued her laser focus on equity and ethics in technology. Two members of Gebru's old Google team, Alex Hanna and Dylan Baker, followed Gebru to her new organization, demonstrating how professional bridges can span organizational boundaries and provide resilience against failure.[28]

So while their bridge had only limited success in creating collective action toward equity at Google, their efforts within their AI work group were more successful and the bridges they created were sustained into further positions with the same goals toward equity. Their actions and responses, and their bravery and willingness to bond together when being treated with unfairness, has also put public pressure on other technology companies to improve their own equity responses. Shared Sisterhood is rarely a straight line toward positive results, but Gebru and Mitchell's example (along with the rest of their Ethical AI team) demonstrates the centrality of bridge building when equity is the goal.

Achieving equity in academia: Adia Harvey Wingfield and WashU

Academia is known to be historically exclusionary toward Black and Latinx/Hispanic men and women. While academic leaders have identified the problem for decades, they have not mobilized the resources to fix it. Yet, one person who practices Shared Sisterhood principles can make a big difference. Dr. Adia Harvey Wingfield put these principles to work in the Sociology Department at Washington University in St. Louis (WashU).[29] The department was restructured in 2015 and is now (as of 2022) composed of nearly 50 percent faculty who identify as people of color. Wingfield, a Black woman, spearheaded the effort to build a diverse department, securing resources and buy-in at the institutional level, including tenure funding, retention packages, and other financial incentives to attract the diverse faculty members she targeted to build the department. She proactively reached out to Black and other candidates of color to encourage them to apply and recruited from professional organizations that focus on diversity in higher education.

Wingfield's institutional risk-taking and her willingness to step out to build a department from the ground up with no guarantee of success demonstrate principles of Shared Sisterhood. Additionally, Wingfield has role-modeled how to be "really intentional" about inclusion during decision-making for members of the department, focusing less on hierarchical forms of power and more on collaborative, inclusive success. Combining interpersonal sisterhood—Wingfield partnered with two White men to build the department, who were on board to support the mission that she envisioned—and institutional support, WashU is one of the most racially and gender-diverse sociology departments in a historically predominantly White institution.

Recognizing Latina political power: Eva Longoria and America Ferrera

Desperate Housewives was a cultural phenomenon of television, and Eva Longoria was one of its breakout stars. Now she is not only well known for her acting and directing chops; she has also established herself as a force in politics. Eva Longoria and America Ferrera are close friends, and, like with the example of Ava DuVernay and *Queen Sugar*, the two look forward to their Sisterhood growing the pie[30] for Latina actresses in Hollywood and making space for everyone to be successful. Together, they transformed this interpersonal Shared Sisterhood into institutional collective action creating one of the first Latina digital community groups, the Poderistas.[31]

Longoria, Ferrera, and Zoe Saldana started She Se Puede in 2020 in response to growing frustration that Latina voters were being taken for granted and lacked confidence in their own power. The trio's goal was to expand their Sisterhood into a larger Latina community, where women could recognize their own political power.[32] The Poderistas is the resulting community—hosting political summits, engaging in digital activism, and building relationships.[33] Will the principles of Shared Sisterhood in action with the Poderistas lead to long-term collective action? We can't wait to find out.

Engaging local communities: A personal story

In 2019, I (Tina) lived an example of Dig, Bridge, and collective action in my own neighborhood. I wanted to find out if Shared Sisterhood would resonate with other women, so in a local moms' online group, I posted a flyer requesting participation in a Shared Sisterhood workshop. A week later, twenty women from different racioethnic backgrounds convened to attend a Shared Sisterhood workshop. During that workshop, women opened up, cried, expressed disappointment, and clamored for more. These women yearned for the type of authentic connection that we were beginning to forge. The workshop was slated to last for two hours; four hours later, we were still talking in the parking lot. A new sisterhood had been established. Afterward,

I created a Facebook group so that the twenty workshop participants would have a way to communicate with each other. In the summer of 2020, in a moment of desperation after learning of George Floyd's murder, I posted a video imploring White women to engage in Shared Sisterhood.[34] As a result of the video, the Facebook group grew from twenty to two hundred to two thousand, and as of 2022, it stands at just under forty-five hundred women.[35]

Members of that initial Shared Sisterhood workshop and I have subsequently come together to engage in collective action in our local community. We have collaborated to ensure that administrative and political appointees have a basic understanding of diversity, equity, and inclusion and that their decision-making reflects our community's shared values around these topics. For example, one potential appointee had failed to consistently honor these values, privately promising that he would uphold the community's values around equity and inclusion but publicly backing down when he was confronted by community members who disagreed with those values. That appointee ended up not accepting the position. The person who was eventually appointed is someone with a long history of privately and publicly supporting our community's values. Right now, our local Shared Sisterhood group is collectively organizing to ensure that our public school system is on par with surrounding communities that employ best practices to ensure that our public schools are diverse, inclusive, and equitable.

You Too Can Drive Collective Action

So far, most of our examples have featured individuals with formal positions of power or celebrity. But we encourage those of you without such positions to consider what other types of power you can garner within your institution. For example, you can build bridges with others who are concerned about the values of diversity, equity, and inclusion. (The sidebar "Getting Started" offers a few options for first steps.) Creating this type of collective action is powerful as it allows you to connect and align with other people throughout your organization who would like to work with you to obtain progress toward your goals.

Getting Started

Starting to act may seem daunting. But little things add up. Here are some things you can do right now to move toward collective action:

- **Connect with others:** Examine your reading lists, your news, and your social media communities. Who do you listen to every day? Challenging yourself can show you areas where your collective action may benefit from further Dig and help you to find communities to join.

- **Build community:** Reach out to colleagues at work and elsewhere who have demonstrated that they share your values of equity. Focus on improving justice and equity at your respective workplaces.

- **Get curious about your organization:** Inquire with human resources about the type of data on recruitment, hiring, retention, and salary they have regarding fairness across groups. If they don't have it, encourage them to collect it.

Collective action is facilitated when we recognize that we need each other because systems of inequity are best dismantled via collective action. As you seek to build these bridges, remember that collective action is most likely to occur when:

1. You and at least one other person recognize that you have not accomplished a desired goal(s).

2. You all are motivated to work with each other to accomplish the goal.

3. You recognize that working together is necessary for goal accomplishment.[36]

Of course, some people are afraid of collective action because they fear a negative spotlight on their behaviors—past or present. Unfortunately, when we focus on negative attention toward ourselves, it can prevent us from being courageous, taking risks, and living into our values. Although we may assume that if we participate in collective action there will be a (negative) spotlight on us, this assumption ignores the power in authentic connection that will be left on the table if we do not act. There is power in numbers and collective action. There is power in the interpersonal and in the collective. There is power in innovating and thinking creatively. Being brave alone may be the best course in certain situations; however, we encourage being brave *together* when confronting and dismantling systemic inequities. Shared Sisterhood is not naive: the power of it lies in bridges. Any one individual cannot take on a system, but all of us, hand in hand, armed with self-awareness, authentic connection, and value alignment? Then we can change the world.

Thinking, Feeling, and Doing

Think

Do you think DuVernay's Shared Sisterhood can be replicated in other places? If so, how? What situations, circumstances, or industries are best for this approach? If not, why not?

Feel

Consider a change that you want to make in your organization to make it more equitable. When you consider acting, how do you feel? Are you scared? Excited? How can you use those emotions to plan your approach?

Do

What are the goals you have for collective action in your workplace? Write down what you want to achieve in terms of equity. Be specific and outline a few ways to get started.

6

Roadblocks to Shared Sisterhood

Since the summer of 2020, we have interacted with thousands of people online about Shared Sisterhood—on Facebook, Twitter, and Clubhouse. During this time, we introduced people to the practices of Dig and Bridge and spent time working through cases and reflections much like what we have introduced to you in this book. We have had many success stories of Dig, Bridge, and collective action, but we have also identified a number of roadblocks that can derail Shared Sisterhood at any of these stages.

Let's take a woman we'll call Joy, for example. Joy, a White woman, attended a public Shared Sisterhood dialogue and engaged with us many times. During one session, she publicly asked a question that stoked racial division: She asked Tina to comment on what White women were getting wrong and asked Beth to comment on what Black women were getting wrong in the Shared Sisterhood process. Immediately, our back-channel direct messages lit up. The discomfort in the room was palpable. We immediately began to redirect the question away from what others were doing wrong, and guided Joy to Dig, in order to re-create the safe space we had created for dialogue and to use the experience as a learning opportunity for Joy. We knew that, if she really wanted to bridge with racially dissimilar people (or, for that matter, other White women who prioritize equity), she needed to understand the impact of the question she had asked.

We asked Joy to dig a bit deeper about why she asked her question in the way that she did. We asked her to see our perspective, but also to learn more about herself so she could grow and set herself up for future bridge opportunities. Joy was uncomfortable with the reframing we provided and became defensive, focusing on her own emotions—she did not, or could not, hear us. This reaction was a further signal to the women in the Shared Sisterhood session that she was not a trustworthy bridge partner. She was blind to this fact and dug in her heels—all the while making the work of Shared Sisterhood more difficult for herself and for everyone in the room.

This example is not an indictment of Joy as a person. She may have truly desired to be a Sister and likely would have identified herself as an ally. But identifying as an ally is not enough when the goal is authentic connection. Joy's failed bridge attempt helps to elucidate the roadblocks that prevented Shared Sisterhood from emerging across the same levels of analysis that we have discussed throughout the book: she may have cared about other people, but she could not see her own blind spots, even with our help. Selfcenteredness and a lack of self-awareness are two key roadblocks that exist at the *individual* level of analysis—they are about what an individual person does (or does not do) to facilitate the emergence of

FIGURE 6-1

Roadblocks at the individual level

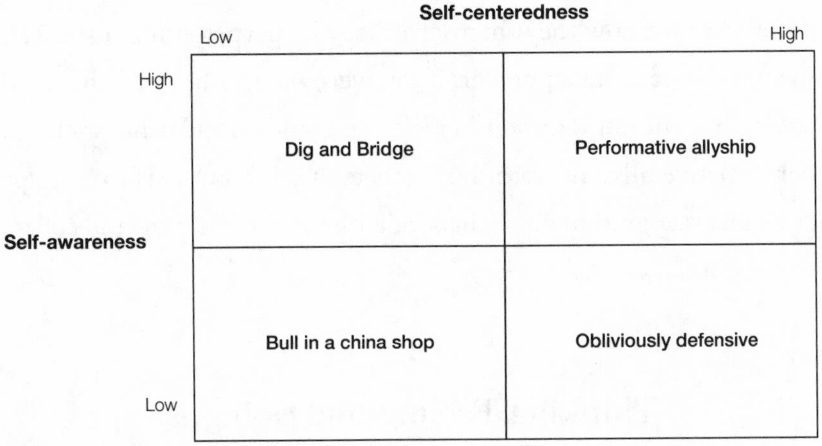

Self-centeredness

	Low	High
High	Dig and Bridge	Performative allyship
Self-awareness		
Low	Bull in a china shop	Obliviously defensive

Shared Sisterhood. Joy's actions also became an *interpersonal* road-block by demonstrating her potential lack of trustworthiness to others from historically marginalized, as well as power-dominant, groups.

For Joy, individual roadblocks were the most significant to over-come in the moment. Consider figure 6-1: in it we place Joy's reaction in the lower right quadrant ("Obliviously defensive")—her individual roadblocks of high self-centeredness and low self-awareness pre-vented her from digging more deeply and from laying the foundation to bridge. To get from where she was to where she could have been, we had encouraged Joy to become more self-aware and to focus less on her own feelings.

Notice, also, that Joy needed to *both* heighten her self-awareness and focus less on her own feelings. If Joy were to only decenter her-self but not heighten her self-awareness, we would characterize her attempts as a "bull in a china shop"; she would mean well, but she

129

would not be ready to bridge because she does not see her own blind spots nor does she demonstrate a deep dig. Women working on Dig and Bridge are often exhausted by people in this quadrant as they do not always see how they themselves may be perpetuating historical, inequitable patterns of power. If Joy were only to heighten her self-awareness but not decenter herself, we could consider her a classic performative ally: aware of how others saw her but performing for clout and recognition more than for authentic connection and collective action.

Thinking, Feeling, and Doing as Roadblock Identification

The good news is that none of these roadblocks are permanent or static—they can be overcome. Throughout this book we have asked you to reflect on what you are "thinking, feeling, and doing." The same exercise can be helpful when scanning for roadblocks—a tool you can use to identify the level at which your roadblock occurs so you can pursue the proper intervention: there are many individual, interpersonal, and institutional roadblocks that could be identified by asking yourself what you are thinking, feeling, and doing in response to situations at work. Each roadblock requires different steps to overcome, and the first step is identifying them.

In table 6-1 we demonstrate how asking yourself what you are thinking, feeling, and doing can help you identify the level of your roadblocks to Shared Sisterhood so you can identify what to do next.

This is not a comprehensive account of roadblocks, of course, as each person's journey will be idiosyncratic to themselves. But this account is demonstrative of how roadblocks can be identified using

TABLE 6-1

Thinking, feeling, and doing as roadblocks

	Think	Feel	Do
Individual	You don't know what you think about your own racioethnicity.	You feel shame at your own reactions to learning about your racioethnicity and social identities.	You refuse to engage in Dig at all.
Interpersonal	You don't think someone is a trust-worthy connection.	You feel angry at a comment a colleague at work made about racioethnicity and that prevents further connection.	You do not act authentically in your connections with a potential Bridge partner.
Institutional	Your organizational culture shuts down questions about racioethnicity and power.	You feel scared to show vulner-ability because your company fosters competition.	Your company makes it difficult for you to speak up in response to inequity.

the very skills you have been honing throughout this book. By examining what you are thinking, feeling, and doing at any given moment in your Shared Sisterhood journey, you can identify whether the source of your thoughts, feelings, and actions is individual, interpersonal, or institutional in nature, thereby allowing you to adapt and grow as you work toward the goals set forth in this book.

Thinking

When we ask ourselves what we are thinking, it includes examining the ideologies and perceptions that may hinder our ability to dig, bridge, or collectively act. These may include prejudices we have, stereotypes we hold, or other cognitive errors that may prevent us from digging into our thoughts about racioethnicity, gender, or power. For instance, using our thoughts as cues can help us to avoid falling prey to attribution errors and self-serving biases, which often cause people to search for external reasons for their own failures and internal reasons for the failures of others.[1] In other words, we tend to grant *ourselves* the benefit of the doubt more than we do for others.[2] Interrogating those thoughts can unveil roadblocks that we can overcome via Dig, Bridge, or collective action.

Feeling

When we ask ourselves what we are feeling, we allow our emotions to be a guide and a signal to what might be holding us back. In Dig, we talked about using emotions as signals. One of the most common emotions that White people have conveyed to us is fear. We've seen similar findings in our research. Sherry Watt's Privileged Identity Exploration Model suggests that the underlying emotion that prevents people from analyzing their own privileged identities in a college environment is fear.[3] This fear—of finding something out that unmoors you, of failing, of not being liked (which, as Ella Bell and Stella Nkomo note, is a common fear that White women have that can interfere with the development of interracial relationships), or potentially even of career backlash—can underlie many roadblocks to Shared Sisterhood as well.[4] Critically, emotions are data points, not facts. For example, Nolan Cabrera's study of White college students found that when men were in academically competitive and racially diverse contexts, they often channeled their fear of losing social status and competing with students from historically marginalized groups into anger—but they felt that their emotional responses were factual assessments, not reactions to racial anxiety, anger, or fear.[5] Recognizing our emotional responses, and being comfortable being wrong, are critical prerequisites for Shared Sisterhood.

Doing

Our actions, and inactions, can also be signals of roadblocks that we need to navigate to engage in Shared Sisterhood. Sometimes our inability to act in ways that would promote Dig, Bridge, or collective action can lead Bridge partners to view us as untrustworthy. Using trust as a guide, we can ascertain whether our actions have violated trust, revealed a lack of trust in the Shared Sisterhood philosophy, or demonstrated that our organizations neither trust us nor are trustworthy themselves. In this way, our actions (and even inactions) can be critical signposts identifying roadblocks we need to overcome.

After using the tool of thinking, feeling, and doing, you can identify the level at which your particular roadblock occurs. In the sections that follow, we describe the most common individual, interpersonal, and institutional roadblocks that we observe in Shared Sisterhood. These roadblocks may affect the emergence of authentic connections in the first place or hinder the ability for those connections to turn into collective action. These examples are not comprehensive—you may experience roadblocks that fall outside of the scope of this chapter. But the principles behind how to identify and overcome such barriers are applicable beyond the specifics we provide.

Individual Roadblocks

At the individual level, roadblocks to Shared Sisterhood focus on the role of the self as preventing Dig, Bridge, and collective action. The most common individual roadblock we observe is an unwillingness on the part of an individual person to be honest about how they actually think and feel.

133

While it was once socially acceptable for White people to express racist attitudes publicly, societal norms have evolved. However, some people may still privately hold these racist attitudes. People might never admit this outwardly (or even consciously) to themselves, but their inner thoughts and reactions demonstrate that they think this way, even if they suppress it. A lack of awareness of your innermost thoughts or an unwillingness to admit them to yourself is a significant roadblock to Shared Sisterhood. This roadblock makes Dig almost impossible: if you uncover your beliefs but then decide to dismiss them and pretend you do not hold these beliefs, you are not authentically learning about yourself and your identities. The beauty of Dig is that it liberates us to uncover what we *actually* think and believe. If people are unwilling, or unable, to honestly consider their thoughts and feelings, it makes it impossible to do the work of Shared Sisterhood.

There are at least two reasons why this is a common roadblock: (1) we want others to see us as we see ourselves; and (2) we have a fear of backlash if we reveal things that others may disagree with.[6] People seek self-confirming reactions from relationship partners in ways that reaffirm how they see themselves.[7] Identities are strong and persistent—whether personal or social. Importantly for Shared Sisterhood, people will seek feedback on their own behaviors more readily when they think the feedback will confirm how they see themselves, which may prevent authentic emotional interaction if someone feels their self-concept and image will be challenged.[8] For example, work by Miguel Unzueta and Brian Lowery has suggested that White people are often motivated to maintain non-racist senses of self and will reframe interactions with racism and inequity in ways that serve their egos.[9] This is why this roadblock—our desire to see ourselves in positive ways, and for others to see ourselves just as positively—can be so pernicious. There are many psychological tendencies that are working against our growth and awareness.

When we discover elements of ourselves that run counter to our self-perceptions, we can feel various emotions about that realization. Emotions are cues that serve as signals for us to understand the roadblocks that are preventing us from digging and bridging. The key emotional cue that is indicative of this roadblock is shame, which can lead to withdrawal, denial, and an overall lack of action to confront and change one's attitudes. Shame results from an inability or unwillingness to accept our mistakes and shortcomings in our past actions or when our self-evaluations do not align with how we want to be seen. If you evaluate your past actions, you may find yourself thinking, "Oh my goodness! I believe racist things! I am racist!" This reaction can prevent the introspection necessary to examine and alter your underlying beliefs and can interfere with the authenticity needed to build bridges with others.

Shame, guilt, embarrassment, and pride are all considered self-conscious emotions that involve, by nature, a form of self-reflection and self-evaluation. Of these, guilt and shame are also moral emotions, connected to our sense of right and wrong.[10] And, although moderate levels of guilt can sometimes lead people to redress wrongs, shame is not constructive. Shame is a critical emotion to avoid because its pain interferes with empathy and leads to denial, defensiveness, and even aggressive behaviors.[11] Shame can also make people more prone to anger.[12] The shame of experiencing a threat to your self-identity of "ally" or "not racist" can prevent anti-racist action, and shame after making a mistake can lead to paralysis instead of needed growth.

It is important to recognize when we are feeling shame and learn from that recognition. When you recognize that you are feeling ashamed, you can use that understanding to explore why you feel shame. Shame can instigate increasing self-criticism and rumination, dwelling on negative emotions over and over again.[13] We recommend identifying when shameful feelings are making you feel defensive or angry, and instead of allowing this emotion to paralyze you, choose to return to Dig to determine why you feel this way. This can be difficult (which is why it is such a common roadblock), but the exercises in this book that have helped you identify what you are thinking and feeling can help you learn the skills to identify shame, fear, or anger before these emotions interfere with your Dig and Bridge practices.

Emotions can serve as a gateway or a roadblock to learning, and we have discussed how fear and shame can prevent us from allowing ourselves to experience the necessary discomfort to promote growth.[14] Relatedly, research on anti-racism suggests that many White people have experienced an uncomfortable triggering event that leads them to either confront their own racist viewpoints or refuse to recognize the triggering event.[15] A refusal to recognize these triggering events or evaluate them critically because of shame may prevent further self-exploration and growth. Take the opportunity to examine the triggering event and choose to continue to dig when you are uncomfortable, as the feeling of discomfort can be a signal that you are doing Dig correctly. As Brené Brown writes in *Daring Greatly*, "We need to cultivate the courage to be uncomfortable and to teach the people around us how to accept discomfort as a part of growth."[16] Too many people equate discomfort experienced during their self-awareness journey with harm or a lack of safety, but remember: growth is only possible when we learn to sit with the discomfort of making ourselves vulnerable.

Interpersonal Roadblocks

Although many roadblocks reside within certain people—in their thoughts and their emotions that prevent Dig or Bridge or collective action—other roadblocks occur between people. Authentic connections are central to Shared Sisterhood because they build a latticework that can lead to powerful collective action. The most common interpersonal roadblock we see among people wanting to enact Shared Sisterhood is a lack of trust in a partner—or being deemed untrustworthy. In chapter 4, we talked about starting to build bridges. Tina noted the importance of determining a person's trustworthiness prior to bridge building and, at times, being hypervigilant for cues of trustworthiness in an attempt to assess riskiness of the potential bridge. This lack of trust can slow down, inhibit, and in some instances, prevent Dig, Bridge, and collective action.

For instance, if I (Tina) decide that a potential bridge partner is not trustworthy, I still will be very pleasant, and I might network with her and even exchange readily available and nonscarce resources. After all, I am a professional. And while I may have decided not to develop an *authentic* connection with someone, I will still engage in necessary interactions to succeed at my work and help my organization. Some people, however, mistake these workplace pleasantries for authentic connection. I have personally experienced White women being overly familiar and intimate with me because they did not realize that I did not reciprocate their sense of closeness. This is one reason that we provided such detail about how to build bridges from the perspectives of members of both power-dominant and marginalized groups.

Know-your-place aggression, a term coined by Koritha Mitchell, is a specific mechanism through which dominant-group members direct anger, aggression, and violence at successful or accomplished members of marginalized groups.[17] And it is not only the direct aggressors who contribute to the mistrust, as members of dominant groups who do nothing in response also contribute, as "those who refuse to upset existing power dynamics are a perpetrator's best allies."[18] This phenomenon, observed many times over in the lives of employees from historically marginalized groups, often leads to an understandable mistrust of White people and people from power-dominant groups who have been the source of racist aggression and perpetrators of passive responses to racism.

Something that we see interfere with building and generating trust interpersonally is a common socialization pattern among White women in the United States. In *Our Separate Ways*, Bell and Nkomo note that the desire to be liked and to not make a fuss among many White women can inhibit the authentic connection that is the foundation of Shared Sisterhood.[19] This overwhelming desire to substitute polite interaction for authentic interaction, and the fear that you may not like—or be liked by—everyone as you do the Dig and Bridge work of Shared Sisterhood is a critical part of the interpersonal roadblock of not trusting (or being trusted by) your partner. If you cannot be trusted to move past your desire to be liked in order to truly understand yourself and your role in the power structure that exists, how can you be trusted as a Sister?

For instance, we have hosted online conversations among women who are interested in Shared Sisterhood in order to work through cases on Dig and Bridge. In one such conversation, a White woman shared how her fear of being criticized or disliked by her coworkers prevented her from speaking up against racism and from engaging in collective action. The group thanked the White woman for making herself vulnerable, because it is important to unearth such genuine fears. However, when White women with more structural power shy away from Shared Sisterhood out of fear of not being liked, women from historically marginalized racioethnic groups may interpret this behavior as meaning that White women are not willing to take risks and do not understand that many Black women, for instance, are disliked at work merely for being themselves. White women's fears, even when expressed authentically, can degrade trust—because what has been shared reflects a self-centered perspective that signals the need for more digging, and signals to historically marginalized people that White women are not quite ready to bridge.

Untrustworthiness can also be communicated via what Sheen Levine and colleagues call the "racial attention deficit," which consists of underestimating, overlooking, or ignoring members of certain groups. They find that, even when it is in their self-interest to learn from their Black peers, White people are less likely to pay attention to their Black colleagues.[20] This lack of attention is a telling sign that someone is not a trustworthy partner and can be indicative of a critical interpersonal roadblock that must be traversed. (For other indications that someone may not be ready to bridge, see the sidebar "Interpersonal Roadblock Warning Signs.")

How can you ensure that you are a trustworthy partner? And how can you work to trust others? Again, using your emotions as a signal, dig down into what is holding you back from enacting the four components of authentic connections: empathy, vulnerability, risk-taking, and trust. Are you afraid? If so, of what? Ask yourself the following questions:

1. *What emotion am I feeling right now?* Fear? Shame? Anger? Each emotion has different implications for blocking your ability to enact Shared Sisterhood.

Interpersonal Roadblock Warning Signs

The pernicious nature of roadblocks is that you may not be able to easily see them in your own life. Here are some common warning signs that you—or someone else—may be creating an interpersonal roadblock to Shared Sisterhood:

- **Downplaying concerns about racism in the workplace.** A colleague might say, "Oh, I've dealt with that before—that's gender, not racioethnicity; you're overreacting"—or the colleague might ask a person from a marginalized group to be patient while pushing their own (power-dominant) agenda.

- **Providing private support but public silence.** This happens when someone is unwilling to stand up for someone around others while demonstrating empathy in private conversation.

- **Engaging in a "pet to threat" scenario.** A colleague may have a positive, embracing attitude when their ideas or opinions are accepted by someone from a marginalized group, but then the colleague demonstrates a negative, rejecting attitude when their ideas are challenged or questioned.

- **Making ignorant or racist comments.** Comments made about any marginalized group or its members can signal that you do not share the values of equity (for example, "I feel so sorry for you. Isn't your hair so difficult?").

- **Expecting someone from a marginalized group to educate them.** Here, an individual may demand a partner's time and patience without showing a willingness to proactively learn on their own. Dig is an individual practice for a reason—and if you need help, leaning on people who are on your same Dig journey instead of asking for someone from the particular marginalized group to educate you is a good choice.

- **Being unwilling to demand systemic data on equity from your organization on behalf of others.** This could include asking for information on salary and promotion data by racioethnicity, by gender, by level and division, and so on. Usually, the issue of equity and accountability is raised by historically marginalized group members. If you do not demonstrate these sorts of risk-taking behaviors, it can be a signal that you are not a trustworthy partner.

- **Blaming systemic inequities on individual behaviors.** Saying things like "Black/Latinx/Asian employees are just not as polished; that's why they don't ascend to the rank of partner" does not indicate that you have engaged in Dig work around those assumptions and expectations.

- **Being a "holiday, not everyday" ally.** Showing up for marginalized group members only on special occasions, such as Cinco de Mayo or Indigenous Peoples Day or Juneteenth, or after a tragic event (such as George Floyd's murder or the murder of Christina Yuna Lee), communicates that you are not thinking about equity in the same way as your colleagues, and such behavior can demonstrate a lack of existing bridges or a need to do more Dig work.

2. *Are these emotions hindering or enhancing my ability to bridge?* Sometimes, when we share anger at inequity, it promotes collective action.[21] But when our anger is at our bridge partner or ourselves, it can hinder the work we need to do to reach our collective goals. Identifying whether the anger is defensive or constructive is a key step. Similarly, many people mistake guilt for shame. But guilt can sometimes be motivating—shame is not. Be honest with yourself.[22]

3. *Am I focusing on myself and my feelings—and should I?* Be careful not to mistake your feelings for facts: your emotions are a signal, but there are many other data points that you can pull from to make conclusions about why you are feeling what you are feeling. People tend to overestimate how much others notice them and their actions.[23] We feel that everyone is paying attention to us more than they are. But when we assume this, we can often feel like we need to overexplain ourselves, or that others are seeing the world the way that we do. Centering our own experiences of fear or anger can lead us away from digging down deeply into the cause of those emotions, and the beliefs that surround them, in ways that isolate us from true connection. And it can prevent an authentic bridge when you're more focused on yourself than hearing and empathizing with someone else's experience. This is particularly true when the person centering themselves is inadvertently replicating patterns of power that systematically disadvantage certain racioethnic groups compared to others. Remember, everyone in Shared Sisterhood must dig and bridge in order to promote collective action. But the burden is

very different based on the history and power structure related to what we uncover.

Given our intentional focus on centering the experiences of people who have been historically marginalized, we have dedicated time to talking about what may serve as a roadblock for Black women, or other members of marginalized groups, from interpersonally connecting with others. But White women and others from historically power-dominant groups may also encounter interpersonal roadblocks.

When I (Beth) attempt to bridge with Black women, for instance, I may encounter some resistance due to the lack of trust we have discussed. Pushing too hard or too fast to connect in these situations, and being unable to adjust the way I interact with others based on this interpersonal feedback, can prevent a bridge from being created. If you want to authentically connect, use your emotional reactions and interpersonal interactions as cues to determine how to proceed. An interpersonal roadblock in this situation is when you may be reluctant to or frustrated at having to change yourself or your approach to facilitate these connections. You may ask yourself: Am I being true to myself or am I being stubborn? Am I being principled or am I being defensive? Sometimes changing your behavior is warranted; other times, it may not be. Some of this seems like an individual roadblock for which Dig can be helpful, but it becomes an interpersonal roadblock when it determines how you choose to engage in Bridge or whether you choose to walk away.

In instances where you may decide that a bridge with a particular person is not feasible in a particular moment, remember that the goal of Shared Sisterhood is collective action toward equity. So, if you believe that you and this person share the values of equity, but that the two of you will not be able to bridge with each other right now, you can make sure that at least this person is not excluded from the work for equity. You can introduce this person to other people who may be able to successfully bridge with them. Shared Sisterhood does not mean that everyone will be able to bridge with everyone else; yet we can facilitate bridge with others so that collective action toward equity can be pursued and accomplished.

Institutional Roadblocks

When we considered what the most critical and common institutional roadblocks to Shared Sisterhood were, we realized that we could list dozens. But what is the common underlying reason for these institutional roadblocks? The pervasive organizational fixation on who we are versus what we actually do is at the root of many institutional roadblocks. In other words, there is a conflict between what many organizations say they value and what these organizations actually do as evidenced by their outcomes, processes, and policy priorities.

Behavioral integrity is the perceived alignment between what managers say and what they do—or the values they espouse and those they enact.[24] When words and deeds do not align, a critical lapse in trust and credibility can develop. The perceived need to satisfy diverse constituencies, one's own values and traits, and poorly integrated change efforts or policies can lead to a mismatch between what managers say and what they do. This mismatch can have detrimental effects on employee trust in their managers and their organization as well.[25]

Organizations in general have similar concerns. Organizational branding leads many companies to espouse strong equity-related values. In the wake of the murder of George Floyd, many companies spoke out about their commitment to racial equity and diversity.[26] But whether those espoused values become reflected in the enacted policies and procedures in the organization is a very different story.[27] Unfortunately, in the ensuing years after George Floyd's murder, organizational change has not occurred at the level and frequency that initial public responses suggested. It appears that many organizations either never meant what they said but did so because of public relations concerns or, if they did initially mean what they said, they lost the will to take actions that aligned with their words.

We've already discussed how an unwillingness to accept one's own culpability in racist systems and structures can impede Dig and Bridge, and how emotions like fear and shame can make it difficult to do the work that is needed to build authentic connections. An institution that is scared to make a misstep, and scared to challenge the status quo, is no less of a roadblock to change. Companies may be afraid of negative media attention or of changes that may affect financial performance or stock price. Or they may be afraid that uncovering racial inequities in their workplace will result in reputational loss or litigation and choose to keep such inequities out of sight and out of mind, even if employees within that company are bringing them to light. Companies all too often run the risk of being caught with a gap between espoused and enacted values.

But why? The fear of exposure does not reflect the fact that it is often as risky *not* to act as it is to do the right thing and challenge systemic racism and sexism. Sometimes roadblocks come when companies describe themselves as politically neutral to avoid the risk of having their actions and policies being labeled as "liberal" or "conservative" and thus alienating stakeholders who consider themselves to be on the other side of the political spectrum. But in an era when anything can be redefined as politically charged, the risk of exposing the divide between your values and your actions should be seen as more serious: there is a risk either way, but at least when you act on your values, you will retain the reputational benefit of authenticity and credibility.

For example, when Timnit Gebru, whom we talked about in chapter 5, identified some of the inequitable structures she experienced while working at Google, the company attempted to adhere to its espoused values rather than accept that perhaps they had fallen short. Organizational leaders fired her soon after she complained about the glacial pace of addressing the inequity she had experienced within the organization rather than addressing her very real concerns about her treatment. How do we reckon with the disconnect that a company proclaiming its values in equity would act in such a way, when an opportunity to become more equitable was available to them? Perhaps the fear of reputational exposure and the fear of change were relevant here. Perhaps know-your-place biases rendered organizational leaders unable to hear Gebru, a Black woman, or Mitchell, a White woman, when they challenged Google's policies and procedures.[28]

Organizational policies that promote gatekeepers who believe that an organization's espoused values are not merely aspirational but are current descriptors of the organization as it currently is, which perpetuates this status quo. The fear of economic or status loss, fear of retribution, and fear that if organizations change the status quo, they will lose who we are, which leads to rigid adherence to that status quo. And rather than focusing on how true diversity and inclusion can yield benefits, organizations avoid the risk, not realizing that they have now exposed themselves to the risk of becoming the very type of inequitable organization that they so vocally speak out against. Thus, when people do enact Shared Sisterhood to try to make change, they may be met with an institutional roadblock as Gebru and Mitchell were.

How can you identify that you are dealing with an institutional roadblock? Some symptoms are listed below:

- *Discouraging critical comments about the company.* Though many companies want to encourage positive company-related talk, like organizational citizenship behaviors, they also often encourage employees to speak their minds at work.[29] But when companies ignore or strike out at employees who provide critical feedback—whether indirectly or directly—it is a sign that it is not a safe place for employees to dig into their racioethnic preconceptions or to share with coworkers in an authentic way. (See the sidebar "Creating Shared Sisterhood–Safe Organizational Cultures" for more on this issue.)

- *Downplaying systemic racial inequities.* You may hear statements like "If we increase diversity, we have to keep an eye on quality." This, an actual statement made by a leader at one of our institutions, is indicative of an attempt to minimize the problem of inequity. Further, this racist statement was met by silence in the meeting despite the attendance of many people who publicly describe themselves as allies. This public statement had a chilling effect and conveyed a strong message that diversity efforts were potentially going to lower quality (when the opposite is true). Statements that reflect explicit and implicit bias against specific groups can demonstrate a non-inclusive culture that can stand in the way of collective action.

- *Focusing on processes at the expense of outcomes.* One important reflection from Ibram X. Kendi's work *How to Be an Anti-Racist* is that policies that focus on racioethnicity can be anti-racist if they lead to equitable outcomes.[30] The distinction between process and outcome fairness has a long history in management research, and when we couch these distinctions in real-world organizational contexts, we can see indicators of what companies actually value.[31] If companies focus on processes that purportedly increase equity but refuse to select metrics that can determine how effective these processes are at driving equitable outcomes, this is a warning sign of a potential institutional roadblock to Shared Sisterhood. The focus on process at the expense of outcomes is a symptom of companies not wanting to uncover evidence of a misalignment between values and actions—or to invest in true change if they discover evidence of inequities.

- *Unwillingness to analyze and act upon systemic data.* When a company has access to equity data on things like salary or promotions, which they can sort by racioethnicity, by gender, by level, and by division, but they do not invest resources in analyzing and acting on such data, it can be indicative of a fear of what they may find if they look closer.

- *Continuing exclusionary practices despite efforts by groups to stop them.* Often it falls to members of historically marginalized racioethnic groups to speak up against workplace inequities. If an organization persists in exclusionary practices despite such efforts (for instance, if they keep creating all-White search committees after being told that this is problematic, delivering all White finalists for job searches despite being alerted to this problem in the past, and so forth), then it is a warning sign that this institutional context may thwart the collective action of Shared Sisterhood.

- *Reliance on members of historically marginalized racioethnic groups to solve inequities while also fulfilling full-time job responsibilities.* Members of historically marginalized racioethnic groups are often tapped to lead diversity, inclusion, and equity efforts in addition to fulfilling their regular, full-time job responsibilities. These "extracurricular" efforts include employee resource groups (ERGs), affinity groups, equity commissions, diversity committees, and other such efforts. These efforts are often uncompensated and undervalued when it comes to promotion and salary increases despite requiring substantial labor. For example, many Black organizational members have dedicated hours of their time, money, and emotional labor to help improve diversity, equity, and inclusion at their organizations. They have done this work without compensation, and often without appreciation. Not only does this work not often receive positive feedback, but it can backfire, with Black employees being labeled as distracted from their core tasks and focusing on less important service roles.

Besides these larger roadblocks, take note of these additional warning signs that your organization or you might be heading in the wrong direction. Beware if you hear someone say anything similar to the items on this list:

- We cannot compete for highly talented people from historically marginalized racial backgrounds. They are in such high demand that we don't stand a chance.

- There is not a sufficient pipeline. We simply cannot find historically marginalized people and get them to apply.

- We do not have the budget, the people, or the time to properly pursue diversity, equity, and inclusion initiatives.

149

Creating Shared Sisterhood-Safe Organizational Cultures

We have shown that the Shared Sisterhood philosophy can drive collective action toward equity. But how do leaders create an environment where Shared Sisterhood can emerge and be rewarded? Lasting collective action toward equity can emerge when leaders create an environment in which employees can actively participate in the practice of Dig and Bridge.

Amy Edmondson's "psychological safety" construct is one of the most promising cultural change approaches for encouraging Shared Sisterhood to emerge in organizations. In her *Harvard Business Review* article, she talks about psychological safety as the "confidence that candor and vulnerability are welcome," and such a workplace is one where people can feel more comfortable engaging in the Dig and Bridge of Shared Sisterhood.[a] Edmondson's work with executives helped them realize that the anxiety they felt about acting openly, in vulnerable ways, did not result in harm and in fact allowed them to take interpersonal risks in their workplace.[b] Taking the idea of psychological safety a bit further, if you're a leader in your workplace, you can consider the following tips toward a culture that can contribute to an institutional impetus for collective action:

- **Have leaders model Dig and Bridge.** Facilitate opportunities for leaders to work through Dig and Bridge exercises like those in chapters 3 and 4, and encourage their employees to do so as well. This signals support for Shared Sisterhood and may encourage leaders themselves to bridge.

- **Create a space where people can fail.** When digging and bridging, people will inevitably make mistakes. Creating a workplace that does not penalize mistakes—while simultaneously making it safe to share and work together—can facilitate Shared Sisterhood. For instance, research by Jack Goncalo and his colleagues found that gender-diverse groups are more creative when they specify how best to communicate within the group because members in the group have less uncertainty around how conversations will go.[c] This essentially removes the risk of sharing more creative ideas and creates predictability around communication. Though some people feel that setting norms around how we talk to people and the words and phrases we use might stifle creativity and innovation, this work suggests that the opposite is true: people want to know how to communicate with people who are different from them, and such norms can make it feel safer for people to connect in new and different ways.

- **Listen.** Tina often encourages people from historically dominant groups to learn to listen more than they speak (Tina follows this advice herself when she is, for example, in a group discussing religious inequities), and this is no less true for people in powerful positions in the workplace. Leaders play an important role, modeling listening skills to employees who are in lower organizational positions. Pausing, not interrupting, and asking probing questions indicating active listening are critical skills to practice. Saying things like "I hear you saying . . ." while repeating back what you've heard, or asking questions like "Could you tell me more about what you are seeing/thinking/feeling?" can help demonstrate the behaviors you want to cultivate in your organization.

- **Attach rewards to metrics related to the facilitation of Shared Sisterhood.** Leaders might be rewarded for improvements in employee perception of the level of inclusiveness in the workplace, and they might be held accountable when these perceptions become more negative. Leaders can ask questions of employees like "How can I improve the culture at work so that you can bring your whole self to work?" and "How can I improve the culture at work so that you can show your authentic self to your coworkers?" You can also include metrics around representation in power-related roles, such as positions in the leadership pipeline and project management.

Shared Sisterhood cannot be forced. But you can create a welcoming space where it can thrive by pursuing collective action even if it makes you uncomfortable: pause, reflect, and return to your Dig skills to understand those feelings better.

a. Amy Edmondson and Per Hugander, "Four Steps to Boost Psychological Safety at Your Workplace," hbr.org, June 22, 2021, https://hbr.org/2021/06/4-steps-to-boost -psychological-safety-at-your-workplace.

b. Amy C. Edmondson and Diana McLain Smith, "Too Hot to Handle? How to Manage Relationship Conflict," *California Management Review* 49, no. 1 (2006): 6-31.

c. Jack A. Goncalo, Jennifer A. Chatman, Michelle M. Duguid, and Jessica A. Kennedy, "Creativity from Constraint? How the Political Correctness Norm Influences Creativity in Mixed-Sex Work Groups," *Administrative Science Quarterly* 60, no. 1 (2015): 1-30.

- This is reverse racism. It harms White men and it is divisive to talk about racioethnicity at all. If you talk about recruiting people from specific racioethnic backgrounds, you are causing division.

If you see any of these warning signs, reiterate that diversity, inclusion, and equity are critical to your success and that you are committed to investing the necessary resources to ensure that you are able to recruit and retain highly talented people.

Following these tips can minimize institutional roadblocks so that Shared Sisterhood is more likely to thrive. It is, however, very important that you accurately determine that the roadblock is *truly* institutional. If you follow this advice and your institution remains largely unchanged, that is not an "easy out" for you. Even in a context of institutional roadblocks, you can continue to Dig and Bridge. Shared Sisterhood is about being honest and authentic with yourself—so be careful not to blame your institution when you have individual or interpersonal roadblocks that are preventing you from connecting. Remember: if you try to crumble the institutional barriers without your latticework of authentic connections to sustain and support you, you may find yourself burned out and frustrated.

Roadblocks that complicate or prevent Shared Sisterhood are everywhere. But critically, the roadblocks we discussed above can be addressed, because where there is a will to engage in Shared Sisterhood, there is a way. But sometimes there may *not* be a will, and Shared Sisterhood requires that you start with a bridge between two willing parties. In the absence of at least two willing parties, the roadblocks may be immovable. And it may be that you are the unwilling party. For instance, if you have read about Dig,

Bridge, and the experiences of historically marginalized and dominant racioethnic groups and still refuse to confront your own racist ideologies, then Dig and Bridge will not be effective. For those readers, we suggest putting this book down and revisiting it when your willingness changes. A triggering event—seeing a colleague face a racist comment alone, hearing a comment disparaging someone's religion or country of origin, feeling the discomfort of seeing someone you care about held back by stereotypes—could provide the opportunity for you to reframe what you have just read.

Are You Ready to Go?

In the end, you need to learn not only to recognize roadblocks to Shared Sisterhood but also to recognize when you have successfully used the Dig and Bridge paradigm to navigate through, or around, them. Table 6-2 shows examples of when to stop and when to go in Shared Sisterhood for members of historically dominant and historically marginalized groups.

Navigating around the many roadblocks to Shared Sisterhood that can emerge is one step. But truly experiencing the potential of Shared Sisterhood requires more than removing obstacles: it requires affirmative, active choices by those of us who want to increase equity at work.

Thinking, Feeling, and Doing

Think
Regardless of whether you are a leader in your current workplace, think about how power is structured within your company. Are some

TABLE 6-2

When to stop and when to go in pursuit of Shared Sisterhood

	Stop	Go
EXAMPLES FOR MEMBERS FROM DOMINANT GROUPS		
Individual	You are scared you will be called a racist if you express your authentic feelings.	You recognize your fear of being judged for your feelings and use it as a signal to examine your beliefs and understand why you think they may be poorly received by the people you are trying to connect with.
Interpersonal	You talk about your "Black friend" as a substitute for empathizing with people from a different racioethnic group.	You recognize that you channel your empathy for people in other racioethnic groups through your relationship with one person and that thinking this way can lead to mistrust. You return to Dig to (a) figure out why you have relied on your relationship with one person as a blanket stamp of approval as an ally and (b) vow to engage with each potential bridge partner authentically, as a unique connection.
Institutional	You use your company/culture/group's norms or traditions to justify its actions in the face of criticism from people from marginalized groups.	You realize that you have not listened to your coworkers because you were afraid of learning that you were benefiting from the same culture that they felt was stifling their ability, and you begin to connect with them in service of collective action toward equity.
EXAMPLES FOR MEMBERS FROM HISTORICALLY MARGINALIZED GROUPS		
Individual	Your attitudes toward members of your own racioethnic group echo internalized biases that you have not thought much about.	You use this realization as a signal that you need to dig into your attitudes about your own racioethnic group and think about how your beliefs may have been affected by historical power structures.
Interpersonal	You are so angry at the racial injustices in the world that you do not want to connect with dominant-group members that you would otherwise want to bridge with.	You recognize that your emotions are signaling to you that you are not ready to engage in Bridge. Instead of pushing forward and potentially damaging future opportunities to connect, you pause and reflect. You keep tabs on your feelings and thoughts to engage in Dig to find the source of your emotions when, and if, you are ready.
Institutional	The culture in the company you work for makes you fear backlash if you were to try to influence the company toward more racioethnic and gender equity.	You recognize that your fear is a cue to identify what you are really afraid of, and you realize that you have to personally weigh the benefit of creating change at your company against the cost of potential backlash. You pursue the path that makes the most sense for you and connect with other coworkers in small, authentic ways to build a network of relationships to create change, rather than pursuing the change on your own. You trust your instinct if you believe that it is not worth it to pursue equity right now in this particular organization. You also pay attention to internal cues that the environment may be unhealthy and it is time to leave.

people granted more power to execute (or prevent) change than others? How could it be restructured? Where does your power lie?

Feel

Amy Edmondson's book *The Fearless Organization* suggests that hierarchical organizations can make employees even more aware of status differences, and less likely to be open and vulnerable. If you are a leader in your organization, how does being in charge make you feel? If you're not a leader, assess your own feelings. Do you feel comfortable sharing authentically in your organizational culture?

Do

Revisit the goals for collective action in your workplace that you wrote down at the end of chapter 5. Using your thinking, feeling, and doing skills, identify an individual, an interpersonal, and a collective roadblock that might make such action difficult and write them down next to each goal. Then jot down some ideas for overcoming them.

7

Calls to Action

In early 2021, Dr. Kim Tran wrote a powerful essay in *Harper's Bazaar* saying that the diversity, equity, and inclusion (DEI) industry had lost its way. As an activist and scholar focused on liberation and transformative justice, she wrote, "The multibillion-dollar juggernaut [of the DEI industry] has left its social justice principles, and the people who established them, far behind. But what would it mean to radically reimagine DEI? To recast it not as a mere shadow, but a reflection of the social protest from which it formed?"[1] For us, Shared Sisterhood is a core component of this radical change.

The Shared Sisterhood philosophy about racioethnic and gender equity at work addresses other criticisms of DEI efforts that have emerged over the past few years. We are not the first to notice that many current strategies have fallen short of their intended goals. In fact, experts who have spent their careers analyzing the DEI efforts of organizations have been discussing these issues for years. For instance, Laura Morgan Roberts, in the 2019 "Big Idea" series on racial justice in organizations on hbr.org noted that there is a gap between what organizations say regarding DEI and what they do.[2] Stephanie Creary's research also speaks to this gap when she found that companies are not very good at assessing whether or not they have accomplished their DEI goals, and thus there are major gaps in the effectiveness of diversity, equity, and inclusion approaches across organizations.[3] In 2016, Frank Dobbin and Alexandra Kalev wrote about why diversity programs fail in organizations, noting that focusing on the negative reasons for diversity programs (for instance, "We will get sued if we discriminate against people from marginalized racioethnic groups") does not inspire converts to equity.[4] Robin Ely and David Thomas concur: a "discrimination and fairness" approach to diversity may inspire representative diversity in a short time period, but not lasting equitable change.[5]

The common denominator in this criticism is that the typical organizational approach to DEI is incomplete and not set up to generate lasting change toward equity. Typical approaches can even *backfire* against historically marginalized employees—for instance, Courtney McCluney and Verónica Rabelo's work demonstrates that many DEI approaches attempt to "manage Blackness" in order to encourage assimilation into White cultural organizational norms.[6] But what is also evident in the expertise of many scholars is that building relationships, encouraging open conversations about racioethnicity and racism, and thinking about DEI approaches across levels of analysis that are idiosyncratic to a particular organization are critical to generating the *outcomes* of equity that many companies overlook.[7]

We are not naive enough to believe that Shared Sisterhood is *the* answer to these criticisms of DEI. But it could be *an* answer for how we can rethink the way in which we create change around racioethnicity and gender and the identities that are imbued with power and status in our society. There will be people of all racioethnicities and all genders in our organizations, and people of color will eventually become the numeric majority in society and in some companies. But, as these experts note, organizations are engaging in DEI efforts that do not create sustained change. And part of the reason is that these organizations still hold a very transactional view of power and what it means to succeed. Even when companies actually employ metrics to evaluate DEI efforts, they are usually metrics of revenue, profit and loss, and turnover—not relationships, connection, and emotion. With Shared Sisterhood, we ask whether the true power to change actually lies in growing and connecting with others and using those connections to foment the dismantling of systemic inequities. We echo Demita Frazier, an original founder of the Combahee River Collective, whose approach to collective action and social change focuses on taking care of one another and fighting for justice alongside others across differences of age and experience.[8]

The principles in this book can help you think about yourself, other people, and the power systems you inhabit in very different ways. We believe in the Shared Sisterhood philosophy that we have presented in this book: it has worked for us, and it can work for others.

Shared Sisterhood from Past to Present

Shared Sisterhood has the power to create long-lasting change toward equity. In 1913, when Ida B. Wells-Barnett and Belle Squire returned from the momentous parade for women's suffrage in DC, they came home to an organization they had founded together to promote Black women's civic participation—the Alpha Suffrage

Club. They used their Sisterhood to create a group that would organize a grassroots effort toward suffrage and engagement, with the express focus to make Black women a force in electoral politics.[9] Together, they set the goal of electing the first Black alderman to preside over the majority-Black second ward in Chicago. Then, after signing up thousands of Black women voters and mobilizing for change, they were pivotal in electing Oscar DePriest as alderman in 1915. In 1929, DePriest became the first Black person elected to Congress in the twentieth century, representing Chicago's 1st Congressional District.[10]

DePriest helped lay the groundwork for Chicago politics to become what some call the mecca of Black American politics. Why? First, Illinois has sent more Black people to Congress (nineteen) than any other state.[11] Second, one of DePriest's successors in Chicago's 1st Congressional District was Harold Washington; Washington first served as a congressional representative and then went on to serve as Chicago's first Black mayor. Third, Washington's political success inspired Jesse Jackson to run for president in 1984, only the second Black American to run for president after Shirley Chisholm's 1972 campaign. Finally, one of the nineteen Black congresspeople from Illinois was Barack Obama, who in 2008 became President Barack Obama, the first Black president of the United States of America.

We know little about how Squire and Wells-Barnett's relationship grew and changed over the intervening years, but we do know that their story inspired celebration and laid the groundwork for actual change.[12] We were astonished to discover this through the line from Wells-Barnett and Squire to DePriest, Washington, Jackson, and Obama. Wells and Squire likely hoped that their Sisterhood would lead to door knocking, registering Black women to vote, and electing DePriest; they likely had no idea that the seed of DePriest's election would lead to such bountiful political fruit. But that is the beauty of Shared Sisterhood. We have no idea how this book may inspire you to forge authentic connections with others, nor do we know how those authentic connections may foster collective action toward equity. What we do know is that neither authentic connection nor collective action will happen if we do nothing. The risk-taking, empathy, vulnerability, and trust that Wells-Barnett and Squire built together formed a connection that exemplified Shared Sisterhood; their legacy, and the legacy of the Alpha Suffrage Club, continues today—in the political structures in Chicago and beyond.

When we think about the promise and possibility of Shared Sisterhood today, we consider other examples of how authentic connections have fueled movements toward equity. The success of many social movements toward change has been largely due to the latticework of authentic connections forged between people of different racioethnic identities.

We think about the story of White women like Virginia Foster Durr, born in 1903 in Birmingham, Alabama. Durr was a dedicated integrationist who worked to end racism with such luminaries as Mary McLeod Bethune, Rosa Parks, and E. D. Nixon. Durr was a member of the Southern Conference of Human Welfare, an interracial organization supported by Eleanor and Franklin Roosevelt and Mary McLeod Bethune that was designed to bring democracy to the South.[13] Durr was friends with Rosa Parks, and it was Durr who introduced Parks to the Highlander Folk School, where Parks learned additional social activist skills that would be needed in the subsequent Montgomery bus boycott. When Parks was arrested for refusing to give up her seat on the bus, Durr, her husband, and E. D. Nixon, a chief architect of the Montgomery bus boycott, bailed Parks out of jail.[14]

Durr's conspiring did not end there. Durr supported the Student Nonviolent Coordinating Committee, housing students, preparing meals for them, and working alongside the students to ensure voting rights for Black people. The title of Durr's autobiography, *Outside the Magic Circle*, refers to Durr's commentary on the three ways that a "well brought-up young Southern White woman" could go. She could comply with Southern expectations and be a *"Gone with the Wind* southern belle."* She could go crazy. Durr chose another route, stating, "Or she could be the rebel. She could step outside the magic circle, abandon privilege, and challenge this way of life. Ostracism, bruised of all sorts, and defamation would be her lot. Her reward would be a truly examined life. And a world she would otherwise never have known."[15] Durr's decades-long commitment to working with Black people to end racism reflects a choice to dig, bridge, and engage in collective action to pursue equity for Black people. Durr demonstrates how White co-conspirators for justice can exemplify the power of Shared Sisterhood.

We think of Black woman activist Florynce Kennedy, who was one of the best-known feminists in the United States in the 1960s and 1970s.[16] Kennedy was a leader in the National Organization for Women, the National Black Feminist Organization, and Black Women United for Political Action. As an attorney, Kennedy arduously worked to protect women's bodily autonomy. She is credited by Gloria Steinem as being a leading force in feminism and organizing, in part because Kennedy served as a bridge between the Black Power Movement and feminist struggles. When schisms developed between the two movements, Kennedy remained steadfast in her assertion that each of the movements would benefit because of the work of the other. Kennedy keenly focused on White feminists engaging in the Black Power Movement.

Similar to the racism that Wells-Barnett experienced from White suffragettes, Kennedy experienced racism from NOW leadership and ended up resigning from the organization in protest. Yet, Kennedy and Steinem continued to work alongside each other via a deep, authentic emotional connection. Kennedy specifically encouraged White feminist activists to engage in what we call Dig and to commit to anti-racist work, inviting them to Black Power conferences to listen and learn.[17] For instance, author Sherie Randolph recalled a time when Kennedy brought two White women to a Black Power conference and Audley "Queen Mother" Moore, the prominent civil rights leader and Black nationalist, demanded that they leave: "Flo said no, they're here to learn and they're staying."[18] Kennedy saw the potential for White women feminists to be students and Sisters—and she facilitated their Dig so that, together, they would be ready to Bridge and collectively pursue systemic equity.

We also recall the action of Domestic Workers United, a multiethnic collaboration of women domestic workers in the state of New York who drove true change via collective action in legislation that codified a "Domestic Worker Bill of Rights" in New York in 2010, spurring change nationally.[19] Building on their legislative success, they launched "Kitchen Table Dialogues" in 2012 to bridge between domestic workers and their employers in honest, authentic conversations about shared values and connection.[20] As former domestic worker Helen Panagiotopoulos wrote, "The unity of domestic workers, working hand in hand with employers is a chance to right a wrong; domestic work is important work—domestic work is real work."

These Sisters are still collectively acting toward equity. Their connections have expanded into national networks, domestic worker centers, and cooperatives, which serve as a foundation for an innovative movement focused on policy change and peer support. For instance, the New York chapter of the National Domestic Workers Alliance is continuing to accomplish their equity goals by bringing women together.[21] You can see it in the law passed in 2021, in New York City, Intro 339, which extended further protections to domestic workers.[22] The collective has also inspired efforts like Care Forward, a grassroots movement of domestic workers in Brooklyn's Park Slope, which aims to raise the standards for domestic workers in their community, and organized peer support, such as We Rise: Nanny Training to empower and motivate domestic workers.[23] The strong bridges that were built in that initial push toward equity were not dissolved upon one legislative success; they were strengthened. This was because they were not built on a transactional goal, but on a transformational one. These Sisters accomplished their goals by bridging across racioethnic, class, and gender differences and, in doing so, provided a model of what is possible when we focus on shared values of equity.

These examples, and the many other examples that we have shared throughout the book, are indicative of the power of authentic connection at the center of collective action for social change. The next steps of Shared Sisterhood will be critical to determining its effectiveness in creating change in workplace racial and gender equity—so what comes next? What can you do to bring Shared Sisterhood to your life, your workplace, and your community? How will you use Shared Sisterhood to create a legacy for yourself and your organization?

An Individual Call to Action

A number of immediate next steps are focused at the individual level. First, it is most important to continue to educate yourself. Shared Sisterhood is an ever-evolving process: the more you dig and bridge, the more you will learn about yourself and others. The ironic thing about education is that the more you learn, the more you will realize what you do not know; your work is never done. Here are a few ways that you can facilitate your ongoing education:

- *Keep reading.* You do not have to re-create the wheel. There are multiple reputable organizations that provide book lists related to dismantling systems of racioethnic and other forms of inequity, and we have referenced many of these resources throughout this book and in our detailed notes. Take the time to read them, scour the books, take your own notes. While reading alone may be insufficient for Shared Sisterhood, it is necessary to facilitate ongoing learning.

- *Follow people from different racioethnic groups on social media.* Most of us gather our information from relatively homogenous racioethnic social networks. Examine your social media feeds—how many people do you follow who are from different racioethnic groups than your own? Following social media feeds from people with different backgrounds provides insight into issues that are important to others—even beyond discussions of racioethnicity or racism—and can provide access to resources that you might not otherwise discover. Shared Sisterhood starts with seeing people who are different from you as fully realized human beings; following others can help you to see their full humanity and learn from their insights.

- *Engage with different news sources.* Include sources both within and outside of the country that you are in, and research the veracity of your news outlets. There are mechanisms that allow you to investigate how biased and accurate your news sources may be, such as Poynter, the world's largest resource and train-ing organization for journalists.[24] We often think of news as being from the right or from the left, but you can benefit from news sources that are focused on different communities and that focus on different issues as well. For example, reading newspapers and magazines founded in Indigenous communi-ties will provide you with different insights on mainstream issues such as environmentalism, health, and social justice. Think beyond the right/left dichotomy and find credible voices to help you understand the experiences of others.

Next, please extend grace to yourself. You *will* make mistakes. You can put plans in place to recognize when you are regressing or revert-ing to prior thought processes or behaviors. One suggestion is to begin keeping a journal. Throughout the development of Shared Sisterhood and the writing of this book, both of us have journaled, and that exercise has enabled us to record our insights and periodi-cally review how our ideas and Sisterhood have developed over time. While none of us will ever reach a state of perfection, with concerted effort we can develop and grow. A journal can help you see this evo-lution and pinpoint problematic thought patterns so you can inter-vene and continue to grow.

Finally—and critically—even while you grant yourself grace to grow and learn, you must hold yourself accountable for the problem-atic thought patterns you discover. Do not accept, excuse, or ratio-nalize them away. Instead, write down the specific steps that you will take to remedy the harmful thinking that you find yourself engaging in. If you do not know where to start, try revisiting the thinking, feeling, doing sections at the end of each chapter. The questions there can prompt you to challenge yourself in important ways.

An Interpersonal Call to Action

Beyond the individual level, you will benefit from taking interpersonal action to create connections and to hold yourself accountable via these authentic connections. To start, we suggest that you:

- *Create book clubs and discussion circles to practice Dig, Bridge, and collective action.* Working through *Shared Sisterhood* with others section by section, chapter by chapter, can help you to think differently about what you have read. bell hooks called out how workshops focused on awareness-building without action can be problematic.[25] You can avoid this problem if you focus your book club or discussion circles on your Dig-related reflections and on building bridges, which can be important tools for enacting Shared Sisterhood. Use the "Thinking, Feeling, and Doing" reflections to guide your conversations. We encourage you to create group norms to ensure that conversations focus on actions rather than solely discussing thoughts and feelings. When creating these clubs and circles, keep in mind that sometimes Dig work is most effective when done with racially *similar* others. This allows people from the same racioethnic groups to tackle Dig work specifically related to their collective's historical context, providing safety for people who are working through racial trauma. When it comes time to bridge, however, conversations with racially *dissimilar* others may help to create authentic connections, and brainstorm and execute collective action.

- *Create a partnership with one other person to hold each other accountable for working toward equity.* Within this partnership, make sure to agree to real consequences for your actions (or inactions). In Katy Milkman's book *How to Change*, she suggests that a key way to drive change is to develop consequences—sometimes painful ones.[26] For example, you might commit to meeting with your accountability partner one time per month, in which you will check in on the to-do list that you have created to apply your learning at work. As a pair, you can determine what consequence for not following through is most motivating.

The power of discussion circles and accountability groups is reflected in one experience that began in the Shared Sisterhood Facebook group. I (Tina) received private complaints from Black women that they were feeling exhausted by the consistent inquiries from White women about how White women could be better Sisters. The Black women didn't feel that the public space in the online Shared Sisterhood group was about them; rather, the group had morphed into a large Dig session for White women. In that moment, I encouraged women from different racioethnic backgrounds to wrestle with this issue in groups with people who were racially similar.[27] As a result, several White women created an accountability group that met for over a year.

Initially, the White women's accountability group met to explore Dig and Bridge. They discussed their personal racioethnic histories, read books, and provided emotional support for each other when they encountered difficulties. A key development was when the women began to apply what they had learned in their accountability group to their workplace interactions. They then returned to the accountability group to share best practices after learning which approaches were most and least effective at work. They did their best to dig and help each other bridge with others of different racioethnicities. Unfortunately, the group began to disintegrate when the members could not agree on how to challenge each other during the practice of Dig—they could not agree on an approach to holding one another accountable. Some of the White women felt that the other White women were not qualified to challenge them. Some of the women wanted to drive change (based on what they had learned from women of color in the larger Shared Sisterhood group, they wanted to be Sisters) while others were content to learn and use that new knowledge if they saw fit (based on their personal preferences, not necessarily input from historically marginalized people, they wanted to be allies). They were at an impasse.

They asked me to intervene, and after speaking with this group I recognized that accountability groups are most successful when they plan ahead. If you want to build an accountability group that enables members to take what you have learned in your groups to your workplaces, you can do so. Considering the following questions can help you to start off on the right path:

- *Who:* Who will you invite to your accountability group? Anyone? Beginners? People with more experience bridging with people who are different from you? Who will lead? How will you determine leadership roles?

- *What:* What will you all discuss? Will you focus on particular topics (for example, education, politics, religion, racioethnicity)? Will you focus on developing action plans to facilitate change? Sharing personal experiences from the workplace?

- *When:* How frequently will you meet? How will you accommodate people who may be in different time zones?

- *How:* How will you handle conflict in your group? Will conflict resolution be based on majority rule? Expertise? Overarching values?

- *Mission and metrics:* What is the purpose of your group? What metrics will you use to determine the extent of your group's success? How will you track accountability?

- *Application:* How will you apply what you've learned in the group to your workplace, neighborhood, other collectives?

- *Documentation:* How will you document your group's progress? This can be essential as you all track your progress and, perhaps, share your insights with others so that they can start their own accountability groups.

By planning ahead, you can use your Shared Sisterhood accountability group as a place to share best practices and learnings, challenge each other, and hold each other accountable for measurable progress and collective action.

As you work to build your interpersonal connections, remember to be authentic to yourself and to others. Sometimes the desire to promote social harmony can lead to concealment that is antithetical to the Shared Sisterhood philosophy. People often conceal parts of their social identities that are considered higher in status when meeting new people because they think revealing higher status identities would threaten social harmony and connection.[28] For instance, someone may pretend that they do not have the privilege that they do. This sort of catering to others' expectations and interests in order to manage impressions with others can backfire, leading to great anxiety and lower group cooperation, compared to behaving authentically.[29] You can practice this by returning to Dig when you recognize yourself doing this—when your desire to connect leads you to obscure your real self. Change is built on the strength of authentic connection; when you build connections that are false in some way, they may not be able to be sustained.

We are aware that for some people our focus on authenticity will be used as an excuse for cruelty. Dig and introspection can help you to identify these tendencies in yourself as you work with others. Former Google leader Kim Scott has demonstrated that what is often praised as authenticity and honesty is actually just someone being unkind.[30] Connecting authentically means being honest with yourself about your thoughts and feelings and considering how your actions will affect authentic connections with others: authenticity does not mean threatening the physical, mental, or emotional wholeness of others. In other words, instead of sharing everything you think or believe, particularly if it may cause harm, Shared Sisterhood asks you to recognize these beliefs and explore them yourself using Dig so that you can connect authentically in a way that advances your shared goals of equity.

An Institutional Call to Action

Many readers will be members of organizations that have a lot of work to do on diversity, equity, and inclusion, and many others will be managers or leaders who hold some sort of positional power within their companies. Our institutional call to action speaks to everyone who works within the boundaries of a company that needs to move toward equity. Organizations are uniquely positioned to help society become more diverse, equitable, and inclusive—if they can move beyond mere platitudes and create actionable and transparent action plans to improve. Beyond thinking about the degree to which your organization has a "Sisterhood-Safe Culture" (see the sidebar in chapter 6 called "Creating Shared Sisterhood–Safe Organizational Cultures"), the following questions map onto broader organizational policies and procedures. You can use these questions as a guide to determine how ready for Shared Sisterhood your organization is.

- *Recruiting.* How diverse, equitable, and inclusive is your current recruiting process? How transparent are your recruiting processes?

- *Organizational socialization.* How do you introduce new employees to your firm? What norms, traditions, and so forth do you emphasize?

- *Managing performance.* How do you manage and grade performance? Who is advantaged and disadvantaged by your company's approach?

- *Training and development.* What systemic training do you have to help your organization? What does it focus on? Is the training voluntary or mandatory? Why?

- *Compensation and benefits.* Do you collect data for salary and promotion by racioethnicity, by gender, by division, and by level to see if you notice any patterns? Can you compare salary levels to performance metrics?

In answering these questions, you will have gathered data about the work that is left to do in your particular organization, and you can do things like:

- Request data transparency, collecting data by racioethnicity and gender by level and division and comparing this data to performance metrics aligned with the equity goal of Shared Sisterhood.

- Create metrics to hold leaders accountable for equity. Include a communication plan to share progress and challenges, and encourage public review of how each group and leader is doing on DEI issues. Make sure that the organization is accountable to historically marginalized employees rather than expecting them to lead the charge.

- Create Shared Sisterhood leader panels and working groups. Beyond the metrics of success, this intermediate action can signal that Shared Sisterhood activities from all employees are welcome.

When developing these action plans, we encourage organizations to shift the emphasis from individual-level solutions—encouraging women to enhance their negotiation skills, or Black employees to improve their networking skills—to collective-level solutions that examine institutional policies, procedures, and norms that contribute to inequities. Charlice Hurst coined the term *"not here" syndrome*, in which people deny that racism is a problem in their own organizations, even when they are willing to acknowledge its prevalence in society.[31] This is similar to what Eduardo Bonilla-Silva refers to as "racism without racists."[32] In other words, even those who may dig deep enough to recognize societal sources of power and prejudice may not be willing to admit that it also is true of their own workplace, especially if they are in leadership positions. Be vigilant for this denial reaction to calls for change. Companies are often bold in their innovation around products, services, and overall organizational strategies—being bold in the service of equity is a necessity as well.

Empowering Ourselves and Each Other
with Shared Sisterhood

Women are tired. If our workplace relationships are so broken and overshadowed by personal biases, interpersonal harm, and systemic racism and sexism that women, and particularly women of color, would rather leave their jobs than return to them, then the problem at hand will not be fixed just by increasing diversity and representation. The way we connect with each other at work and the policies and systems that we create need to be addressed.

The good news is that when we have outlined the Shared Sisterhood model with women, their eyes have lit up with hope, because the Shared Sisterhood philosophy coupled with the practice of Dig and Bridge provides a path to personal knowledge, interpersonal connection, and collective action. Because it is a philosophy that emphasizes the uplift and respect of all women, Shared Sisterhood is a balm, a solution that fosters hope and helps dismantle systems of inequity via collective action.

This book has been a true labor of Shared Sisterhood, demonstrating the power of authentic connection. May Miller, the most widely published woman playwright of the Harlem Renaissance, once said, "I am where I am because of the bridges that I crossed. Sojourner Truth was a bridge. Harriet Tubman was a bridge. Ida B. Wells was a bridge. Madam C. J. Walker was a bridge. Fannie Lou Hamer was a bridge."[33] While we would never compare ourselves to such luminaries, we hope that this book will serve as a bridge, a bridge from where we are to where we can be, a bridge from historical to contemporary times, a bridge from inequity to equity for all of us. With that in mind, we will repeat the rallying cry of the feminist movement: "Don't agonize, organize."[34]

What we are experiencing as a society is an opportunity to close the gap between what organizations proclaim to value about work and workers—like equity, inclusion, and justice—and what they actually do to ensure that those values are alive in their company. At this time of great tumult, we encourage you to get introspective about issues of inequity that have long plagued workplaces and to confront the obstacles that emerge whenever you try to close those divides.

We have shared dozens of stories throughout the book, bolstered by the research that guides our work. You have learned about positive examples of Shared Sisterhood, such as the stories of Ida B. Wells-Barnett, Belle Squire, and Virginia Brooks; and Virginia Durr, Florynce Kennedy, and Gloria Steinem. You've learned about some examples where people struggled to work in Shared Sisterhood, stories like those of Joy, the women we surveyed in our HBR research, and the White women's accountability groups. Hopefully, you have learned from these stories. Now we ask: What stories will you write?

Ultimately, we want to hear from *you*. When we think about what Shared Sisterhood can do, we think about what stories we want to be able to tell next. How will you take the Shared Sisterhood philosophy and make it your own? How will you use Shared Sisterhood and the practice of Dig and Bridge to learn more about your own assumptions and biases; to connect with people who are different from you; to forge collective action with your new Sisters? We want to hear about the multiracial group of male coworkers who use their authentic connections to get corrective raises for the women in their company—recognizing that they are stronger when they bridge together than when they try to pursue this solution alone. We want to hear about the White male executive who, after reading this book, asks his VPs to provide metrics on the racial and gender equity in his organization and holds himself—and them—accountable for changing the statistics, recognizing his role in creating a culture where Shared Sisterhood can thrive. We want to hear about the Black woman whose Dig skills allow her to grow in her understanding of her own relationships at work, and the White woman who sees herself in our example of Joy and hones her Dig skills to become more self-aware and ready to bridge. We want to hear stories about Asian, Latinx/ Hispanic, Indigenous, and Middle Eastern women who build upon this foundation of Shared Sisterhood by applying it to their own racioethnic contexts. We want to hear stories from all of you about recognizing the need to add more "doing" to your "thinking and feeling" and that your Dig practice is only as valuable as your desire to bridge and act.

Imagine if instead of traumatizing headline after traumatizing headline, we could see stories hailing more equitable, more just, and more inclusive workplaces. If we all use the philosophy of Shared Sisterhood to dig, bridge, and create equity in our workplaces and communities, what sort of world might we build? When it comes to creating equity, it may be easier to expect others to save the day, but in Shared Sisterhood, we rely on a community of Sisters, a community that *you* can start. If not you, who? If not now, when?

Notes

Preface

1. Kim McLarin, "Can Black Women and White Women Be True Friends?" *Washington Post*, March 29, 2019, https://www.washingtonpost.com/nation/2019/03/29/can-black-women-white-women-be-true-friends/.

2. We purposefully use the terms "historically dominant" and "historically marginalized" to refer to the racioethnic groups throughout the book. Doing so recognizes the ways in which race has been constructed over time and avoids terms like "majority" and "minority," which are often numerical misnomers: what matters more to us is the representation of people with power than the overall number of people in groups.

3. Vanessa Fuhrmans, "Where Are All the Women CEOs?" *Wall Street Journal*, February 6, 2020, https://www.wsj.com/articles/why-so-few-ceos-are-women-you-can-have-a-seat-at-the-table-and-not-be-a-player-11581003276.

4. Ellen McGirt and Aric Jenkins, "Where Are All the Black CEOs?" *Fortune*, February 4, 2021, https://fortune.com/2021/02/04/black-ceos-fortune-500/.

5. Daniel Kurt, "Corporate Leadership by Race," Investopedia, updated February 28, 2022, https://www.investopedia.com/corporate-leadership-by-race-5114494; and Crist|Kolder Associates, "Crist|Kolder Associates Volatility Report 2021," https://www.cristkolder.com/media/2819/volatility-report-2021-americas-leading-companies.pdf. See also Emma Hinchliffe, "The Female CEOs on This Year's *Fortune* 500 Just Broke Three All-Time Records," *Fortune*, June 2, 2021, https://fortune.com/2021/06/02/female-ceos-fortune-500-2021-women-ceo-list-roz-brewer-walgreens-karen-lynch-cvs-thasunda-brown-duckett-tiaa/; and Richard L. Zweigenhaft, "Diversity among *Fortune* 500 CEOs from 2000 to 2020: White Women, Hi-Tech South Asians, and Economically Privileged Multilingual Immigrants from Around the World," whorulesamerica.net, January 2021, https://whorulesamerica.ucsc.edu/power/diversity_update_2020.html.

6. See "bell hooks on Interlocking Systems of Domination," YouTube, January 7, 2018, https://www.youtube.com/watch?v=sUpY8PZlgV8; bell hooks, *Feminism Is for Everybody* (Cambridge, MA: South End Press, 2000).

7. bell hooks, *Belonging: A Culture of Place* (New York: Routledge, 2009).

8. The term "racioethnicity" was used by Dr. Taylor Cox in a seminal 1991 article "The Multicultural Organization," *The Executive* 5, no. 2 (1991): 34–47. Racioethnicity is

defined as race and culture and encompasses such identities as Black/African American, White, Native/Indigenous, Hispanic, Asian, Middle Eastern, multicultural, and others.

9. Carlos Hoyt Jr., "The Pedagogy of the Meaning of Racism: Reconciling a Discordant Discourse," *Social Work* 57, no. 3 (July 2012): 225–234, https://www.jstor.org/stable/23719752; Ibram X. Kendi, *How to Be an Antiracist* (New York: One World, 2019), https://www.ibramxkendi.com/how-to-be-an-antiracist.

10. Euan Lawson, "Prejudice Plus Power = Racism," *British Journal of General Practice* 70, no. 697 (August 2020): 371, https://bjgp.org/content/70/697/371.2.

11. David T. Wellman, *Portraits of White Racism* (Cambridge: Cambridge University Press, 1993), https://www.cambridge.org/core/books/portraits-of-white-racism/B63FB 0737E11F8907AC2643F8D079346; Maurianne Adams, Lee Anne Bell, and Pat Griffin, eds., *Teaching for Diversity and Social Justice*, 2nd ed. (New York: Routledge, 2007), https://psycnet.apa.org/record/2007-13915-000; Robin DiAngelo, "What Is Racism?" *Counterpoints* 398 (2012): 87–103, https://www.jstor.org/stable/42981487; Jenny Bhatt, review of Ijeoma Oluo, *So You Want to Talk about Race* (New York: Seal Press, 2018), *National Book Review*, https://www.thenationalbookreview.com/features/2018/2/1/pzq 0lfjcpd3klmi89d5qinpawx15tr.

Chapter 1

1. See David Dismore, "Live-Blogging Women's History: March 3, 1913," *Ms.* magazine, March 3, 2011, https://msmagazine.com/2011/03/03/live-blogging-womens -history-march-3-1913/, for a detailed write-up (with figures and images) about this march.

2. More information from the White House archives about the women's suffrage parade in Washington in 1913 can be found here: Danielle Cohen, "This Day in History: March 13, 1913," The White House, March 3, 2016, https://obamawhitehouse.archives .gov/blog/2016/03/03/this-day-history-1913-womens-suffrage-parade.

3. Ms. Wells-Barnett's writings occurred in a context where lynching was a tool employed by White individuals to enforce the racial hierarchy. From 1900 to 1920, there were 1,569 lynchings in the United States; 90 percent of the lynchings were committed against Black people. According to a 2017 report by the Equal Justice Initiative, "Terror lynchings in the American South were not isolated hate crimes committed by rogue vigilantes. Lynching was targeted racial violence at the core of a systematic campaign of terror perpetrated in furtherance of an unjust social order." [Equal Justice Initiative, "Lynching in America: Confronting the Legacy of Racial Terror," 3rd ed. (Montgomery, AL: Equal Justice Initiative, 2017), https://lynchinginamerica.eji.org/report/]. Lynchings were not merely wielded by White men against men and women of color: many of the lynchings that Wells-Barnett wrote about were instigated by the false testimony of White women. Understandably, the intra-gender racial divide was large.

4. The gulf of societal anti-Black attitudes that White and Black women had to bridge to enact Sisterhood in 1913 was large. In addition to lynchings, Black people were subjected to White supremacist narratives and policies. For example, President Wilson premiered the White supremacist movie *Birth of a Nation* at the White House— the first movie premiere hosted there. When speaking of *Birth of a Nation*, Wilson reportedly stated, "It's like writing history with lightning. My only regret is that it is all so terribly true." (https://dailyhistory.org/Did_Woodrow_Wilson_state_that_the_film _The_Birth_of_Nation_was_%22like_writing_history_with_lightning%27). The

symbolism of the White House choosing this as its first movie premiere illuminates the pervasive anti-Black attitudes of the time. Additionally, US law reflected White supremacist viewpoints. For example, in 1913, during Wilson's first presidential term, interracial marriage was criminalized in the District of Columbia, the capital of the United States. Wilson institutionalized racial segregation in the federal civil service, requiring that federal job applicants include photo identification so that the racioethnicity of applicants would be apparent and Black people could be barred. Wilson also fired fifteen out of seventeen Black federal employees who had been appointed during the Taft Administration.

5. See the conversation that two women have about their podcast regarding race and social justice work. Nicole Smith, "But Can We Work Together Though? A Black Woman and a White Woman Get Real," Rethink Together, July 28, 2020, https:// xqsuperschool.org/rethinktogether/interracial-collaboration-social-justice; Ella Bell Smith and Stella M. Nkomo, *Our Separate Ways: Black and White Women and the Struggle for Professional Identity* (Boston: Harvard Business School Press, 2003). This book is a foundational work on Black and White women's relationships at work, and we refer to it regularly in our research and practice.

6. Vanessa Fuhrmans, "Where Are All the Women CEOs?" *Wall Street Journal*, February 6, 2020, https://www.wsj.com/articles/why-so-few-ceos-are-women-you-can -have-a-seat-at-the-table-and-not-be-a-player-11581003276.

7. Alice H. Eagly and Steven J. Karau, "Role Congruity Theory of Prejudice toward Female Leaders," *Psychological Review* 109, no. 3 (2002): 573; Ashleigh Shelby Rosette, Geoffrey J. Leonardelli, and Katherine W. Phillips, "The White Standard: Racial Bias in Leader Categorization," *Journal of Applied Psychology* 93, no. 4 (2008): 758; Ashleigh Shelby Rosette, Christy Zhou Koval, Anyi Ma, and Robert Livingston, "Race Matters for Women Leaders: Intersectional Effects on Agentic Deficiencies and Penalties," *Leadership Quarterly* 27, no. 3 (2016): 429–445.

8. For instance, Anna Shaw, quoted above as the leader of the National American Women's Suffrage Association, saw the fight for the right to vote as a competition, lamenting that Black men were granted the right to vote before White women.

9. Corinne A. Moss-Racusin, "Male Backlash: Penalties for Men Who Violate Gender Stereotypes," in *Gender in Organizations: Are Men Allies or Adversaries to Women's Career Advancement?* Edited by Ronald J. Burke and Debra A. Major, 247–269 (Northampton, MA: Edward Elgar, 2014), https://doi.org/10.4337/9781781955703 .00021; Eagly and Karau, "Role Congruity Theory of Prejudice toward Female Leaders," 573.

10. Angelica Leigh and Shimul Melwani, "Am I Next? The Spillover Effects of Mega-Threats on Avoidant Behaviors at Work," *Academy of Management Journal* (February 9, 2022).

11. "Introduction," *Frontline*, PBS, January 1, 2003, https://www.pbs.org/wgbh /frontline/article/introduction-2/.

12. Cameron Anderson and Dacher Keltner, "The Role of Empathy in the Formation and Maintenance of Social Bonds," *Behavioral and Brain Sciences* 25, no. 1 (2002): 21, https://doi.org/10.1017/S0140525X02230010.

13. See President Barack Obama's statement on Trayvon Martin's death here: https://obamawhitehouse.archives.gov/the-press-office/2013/07/19/remarks -PRESIDENT-TRAYVON-MARTIN.

14. Mark H. Davis, "Measuring Individual Differences in Empathy: Evidence for a Multidimensional Approach," *Journal of Personality and Social Psychology* 44, no. 1 (1983): 113–126, https://doi.org/10.1037/0022-3514.44.1.113.

15. Nathan Harris, Lode Walgrave, and John Braithwaite, "Emotional Dynamics in Restorative Conferences," *Theoretical Criminology* 8, no. 2 (2004): 191–210, https://www.anu.edu.au/fellows/jbraithwaite/_documents/Articles/Emotional%20Dynamics%20in%20Restorative%20Conferences.pdf. Juan M. Madera, Jack A. Neal, and Mary Dawson, "A Strategy for Diversity Training: Focusing on Empathy in the Workplace," *Journal of Hospitality and Tourism Research* 35, no. 4 (2011): 469–487, https://doi.org/10.1177/1096348010382240.

16. Salvatore Zappalà, "Perspective Taking in Workplaces," *Journal for Perspectives of Economic Political and Social Integration* (2014): 55–70, DOI: 10.2478/v10241-012-0007-5.

17. See Natalie H. Longmire and David A. Harrison, "Seeing Their Side Versus Feeling Their Pain: Differential Consequences of Perspective-Taking and Empathy at Work," *Journal of Applied Psychology* 103, no. 8 (2018): 894, https://doi.org/10.1037/apl0000307; and Martin Lamothe et al., "To Be or Not to Be Empathic: The Combined Role of Empathic Concern and Perspective Taking in Understanding Burnout in General Practice," *BMC Family Practice* 15, no. 15 (2014), https://doi.org/10.1186/1471-2296-15-15, for more information on the many connections between perspective-taking and empathy.

18. Brené Brown, *Daring Greatly: How the Courage to Be Vulnerable Transforms the Way We Live, Love, Parent and Lead* (New York: Avery, 2013), chapter 2.

19. Nicholay Gausel, Vivian L. Vignoles, and Colin Wayne Leach, "Resolving the Paradox of Shame: Differentiating among Specific Appraisal-Feeling Combinations Explains Pro-Social and Self-Defensive Motivation," *Motivation and Emotion* 40 (2016): 118–139, https://doi.org/10.1007/s11031-015-9513-y.

20. Nicolay Gausel and Colin Wayne Leach, "Concern for Self-Image and Social Image in the Management of Moral Failure: Rethinking Shame," *European Journal of Social Psychology* 41, no. 4 (2011): 468–478, https://doi.org/10.1002/ejsp.803.

21. Deborah S. Froling, "Making Yourself Vulnerable Has Its Advantages; Opening Yourself to Others Broadens and Deepens Your Connection," *Women Lawyers Journal* 98, no. 1–2 (2013): 54, https://heinonline.org/HOL/LandingPage?handle=hein.journals/wolj98&div=7&id=&page=.

22. Frances Frei and Anne Morriss, *Unleashed: The Unapologetic Leader's Guide to Empowering Everyone around You* (Boston: Harvard Business Review Press, 2020). Frei and Morriss offer helpful insights into how trust develops. Additionally, they discuss "trust wobbles," which points out how trust can be weakened and, hopefully, restored.

23. John K. Butler Jr. and R. Stephen Cantrell, "A Behavioral Decision Theory Approach to Modeling Dyadic Trust in Superiors and Subordinates," *Psychological Reports* 55, no. 1 (1984): 19–28, https://doi.org/10.2466/pr0.1984.55.1.19.

24. Paul L. Schindler and Cher C. Thomas, "The Structure of Interpersonal Trust in the Workplace," *Psychological Reports* 73, no. 2 (1993): 563–573, https://doi.org/10.2466/pr0.1993.73.2.563.

25. Kurt T. Dirks, "The Effects of Interpersonal Trust on Work Group Performance," *Journal of Applied Psychology* 84, no. 3 (1999): 445, DOI: 10.1037/0021-9010.84.3.445; Taiki Takahashi et al., "Interpersonal Trust and Social Stress-Induced Cortisol Elevation," *Neuroreport* 16, no. 2 (2005): 197–199.

26. Roy J. Lewicki, Edward C. Tomlinson, and Nicole Gillespie, "Models of Interpersonal Trust Development: Theoretical Approaches, Empirical Evidence, and Future Directions," *Journal of Management* 32, no. 6 (2006): 991–1022, https://doi.org/10.1177/0149206306294405.

27. Lewicki, Tomlinson, and Gillespie, "Models of Interpersonal Trust Development," 991–1022.

28. Roderick M. Kramer and Tom R. Tyler, eds. *Trust in Organizations: Frontiers of Theory and Research* (Los Angeles: Sage, 1995) offers a detailed explanation of the research on trust in companies, and how it develops.

29. Daniela Gachago, "Lessons on Humility: White Women's Racial Allyship in Academia," in *Feminism and Intersectionality in Academia*, edited by Stephanie Shelton, Jill Flynn, and Tanetha Grosland, 131–144 (Cham, Switzerland: Palgrave Macmillan, 2018), https://doi.org/10.1007/978-3-319-90590-7_12.

30. Jane Coaston, "The Intersectionality Wars," Vox.com, May 28, 2019, https://www.vox.com/the-highlight/2019/5/20/18542843/intersectionality-conservatism-law-race-gender-discrimination.

Chapter 2

1. Elizabeth Harris, "People Are Marching Against Racism. They're Also Reading About It," *New York Times*, June 5, 2020, https://www.nytimes.com/2020/06/05/books/antiracism-books-race-racism.html.

2. In 2019, leading scholars on diversity, equity, and inclusion contributed to a special HBR series that delved into the problems with current DEI practices. All five essays are worth reading in full: "Toward a Racially Just Workplace" (The Big Idea Series/Advancing Black Leaders), hbr.org, November 14, 2019, https://hbr.org/2019/11/toward-a-racially-just-workplace.

3. Derald Wing Sue, *Microaggressions in Everyday Life: Race, Gender, and Sexual Orientation* (Hoboken, NJ: Wiley, 2010).

4. Shelley D. Dionne et al., "Diversity and Demography in Organizations: A Levels of Analysis Review of the Literature," in *Multi-Level Issues in Organizational Behavior and Processes (Research in Multi-Level Issues, Vol. 3)*, edited by Francis J. Yammarino and Fred Dansereau, (Bingley, UK: Emerald, 2005): 181–229, https://doi.org/10.1016/S1475-9144(04)03009-7.

5. Winters Group, "There's Levels to This: The Risk of Knowing Your Truth," *The Inclusion Solution* (blog), May 3, 2018, http://www.theinclusionsolution.me/theres-levels-risk-knowing-truth-systems-equity/.

6. Lacey Rose, "Ellen Pompeo, TV's $20 Million Woman, Reveals Her Behind-the-Scenes Fight for 'What I Deserve,'" *Hollywood Reporter*, January 17, 2018, https://www.hollywoodreporter.com/features/ellen-pompeo-tvs-20-million-woman-reveals-her-behind-scenes-fight-what-i-deserve-1074978.

7. Halle Kiefer, "Chadwick Boseman Took a Pay Cut to Increase Sienna Miller's *21 Bridges* Salary," *Vulture*, September 28, 2020, https://www.vulture.com/2020/09/chadwick-boseman-took-pay-cut-to-raise-sienna-miller-salary.html.

8. "Octavia Spencer: 'Jessica Chastain Helped Me Earn Five Times My Asking Salary,'" BBC.com, January 25, 2018, https://www.bbc.com/news/entertainment-arts-42819003; Janet W. Lee, "Why Jessica Chastain Founded Freckle Films and Made 'The

355.'" *Variety* October 29, 2020, https://variety.com/2020/film/news/jessica-chastain-freckle-films-the-355-1234818174/.

9. You'll notice that we include multiple collectives here in the form of both the "organization" and "society" to demonstrate that, while they're both at the collective level, they still represent unique perspectives to consider. While this book is mostly focused on solutions based on the organizational collective, and action of groups of individuals within such organizations, collective solutions can take many forms. In the future, we hope that policy makers will use the foundations developed in this book to develop society-level solutions to dismantle inequities.

Chapter 3

1. Henri Tajfel, John C. Turner, William G. Austin, and Stephen Worchel, "An Integrative Theory of Intergroup Conflict," *Organizational Identity: A Reader* 56, no. 65 (1979): 9780203505984-16.

2. Naomi Ellemers and S. Alexander Haslam, "Social Identity Theory," in *Handbook of Theories of Social Psychology*, vol. 2, edited by Paul A. M. Van Lange, Arie W. Kruglanski, and E. Tori Higgins (Thousand Oaks, CA: Sage, 2012), 379–398.

3. Ellemers and Haslam, "Social Identity Theory," 379–398; Donald M. Taylor and Fathali M. Moghaddam, *Theories of Intergroup Relations: International Social Psychological Perspectives* (Westport, CT: Praeger, 1994).

4. Michael Hughes, K. Jill Kiecolt, Verna M. Keith, and David H. Demo, "Racial Identity and Well-Being among African Americans," *Social Psychology Quarterly* 78, no. 1 (2015): 25–48.

5. Jean S. Phinney and Steve Tarver, "Ethnic Identity Search and Commitment in Black and White Eighth Graders," *Journal of Early Adolescence* 8, no. 3 (1988): 265–277.

6. Eric D. Knowles, Brian S. Lowery, Rosalind M. Chow, and Miguel M. Unzueta, "Deny, Distance, or Dismantle? How White Americans Manage a Privileged Identity," *Perspectives on Psychological Science* 9, no. 6 (2014): 594–609.

7. Robert M. Sellers et al., "Multidimensional Model of Racial Identity: A Reconceptualization of African American Racial Identity," *Personality and Social Psychology Review* 2, no. 1 (1998): 18–39, https://journals.sagepub.com/doi/10.1207/s15327957pspr0201_2.

8. Glennon Doyle, *Untamed* (New York: Dial, 2020), 213.

9. Doyle, *Untamed*, 218.

10. bell hooks, "Sisterhood: Political Solidarity between Women," *Feminist Review* 23, no. 1 (1986): 125–138.

11. It is important to note that Tina's Dig was specifically related to her interpersonal connection with Beth and may not transfer over to other potential Dig partners.

Chapter 4

1. If you begin with friendship rather than authentic connection, that's okay. Sometimes friendships facilitate later authentic connection, because interracial friendships may help White friends develop more empathy for Black people, leading to anti-racist behaviors; and Black friends may experience more hopefulness about other White people in general. See Belle Rose Ragins and Kyle Ehrhardt, "Gaining

Perspective: The Impact of Close Cross-Race Friendships on Diversity Training and Education," *Journal of Applied Psychology* 106, no. 6 (2021): 856–881, https://doi.org/10.1037/apl0000807.

2. Jessica R. Methot et al., "Office Chitchat as a Social Ritual: The Uplifting yet Distracting Effects of Daily Small Talk at Work," *Academy of Management Journal* 64, no. 5 (2021): 1445–1471.

3. John Paul Stephens, Emily Heaphy, and Jane E. Dutton, "High-Quality Connections," in *The Oxford Handbook of Positive Organizational Scholarship*, edited by Kim S. Cameron and Gretchen M. Spreitzer, 385–399 (Oxford: Oxford University Press, 2012).

4. Jane E. Dutton and Emily D. Heaphy, "The Power of High-Quality Connections," *Positive Organizational Scholarship: Foundations of a New Discipline* 3 (2003): 263–278.

5. See Timothy P. Munyon et al., "The Implications of Coalition Forms for Work Role Innovation, Resource Reallocation, and Performance," *Research in Personnel and Human Resource Management* 32 (2014): 65–97.

6. Amy J. C. Cuddy, Susan T. Fiske, and Peter Glick, "Warmth and Competence as Universal Dimensions of Social Perception: The Stereotype Content Model and the BIAS Map," *Advances in Experimental Social Psychology* 40 (2008): 61–149; Melissa J. Williams and Larissa Z. Tiedens, "The Subtle Suspension of Backlash: A Meta-Analysis of Penalties for Women's Implicit and Explicit Dominance Behavior," *Psychological Bulletin* 142, no. 2 (2016): 165.

7. Loriann Roberson and Carol T. Kulik, "Stereotype Threat at Work," *Academy of Management Perspectives* 21, no. 2 (2007): 24–40.

8. Lincoln Quillian and Mary Campbell, "Segregation Forever? Racial Composition and Multiracial Friendship Segregation in American Schools," ERIC (2001), https://eric.ed.gov/?id=ED460207.

9. Kimberley A. Scott, "V. African-American–White Girls' Friendships," *Feminism and Psychology* 14, no. 3 (2004): 383–388, https://doi.org/10.1177/0959353504044639.

10. Dorothy Granger, "Friendships between Black and White Women," *American Behavioral Scientist* 45, no 8. (2002): 1208–1213.

11. See Kiara L. Sanchez, David A. Kalkstein, and Gregory M. Walton, "A Threatening Opportunity: The Prospect of Conversations about Race-Related Experiences between Black and White Friends," *Journal of Personality and Social Psychology*, advance online publication, https://doi.org/10.1037/pspi0000369. Beverly Tatum's book *Can We Talk About Race?* (Boston: Beacon, 2007) is also a good source for the various discomforts that talking about race can cause, particularly among people in historically dominant groups.

12. Jessica Isom, "When Antiracism Becomes Trauma," *Medium*, December 29, 2020, https://jisommdmph.medium.com/when-antiracism-becomes-trauma-77922b188ebb.

13. While the term *virtue signaling* is often thrown around to refer to any comment that is pro–social justice, the term is more precisely applied to "behavior that indicates support for causes or sentiments that carry moral value, *without much actual effort or care for the topic behind it.*" Tracie Farrell, Genevieve Gorrell, and Kalina Bontcheva, "Vindication, Virtue, and Vitriol," *Journal of Computational Social Science* 3, no. 2 (2020): 401–443; italics added. It may also be referred to as "moral grandstanding." Justin Tosi and Brandon Warmke, "Moral Grandstanding," *Philosophy and Public Affairs*

44, no. 3 (2016): 197–217. See also Elaine Wallace, Isabel Buil, and Leslie De Chernatony, "'Consuming Good' on Social Media: What Can Conspicuous Virtue Signaling on Facebook Tell Us about Prosocial and Unethical Intentions?" *Journal of Business Ethics* 162, no. 3 (2020): 577–592.

14. Sanchez, Kalkstein, and Walton, "A Threatening Opportunity."

15. Sun Hyun Park and James D. Westphal, "Social Discrimination in the Corporate Elite: How Status Affects the Propensity for Minority CEOs to Receive Blame for Low Firm Performance," *Administrative Science Quarterly* 58, no. 4 (2013): 542–586; Miles Hewstone, "The 'Ultimate Attribution Error'? A Review of the Literature on Intergroup Causal Attribution," *European Journal of Social Psychology* 20, no. 4 (1990): 311–335.

16. We focus here on Collier's findings regarding Black and White women because of Beth's story, but the article in question discusses college friends of different racioethnicities as well, including Asian and Hispanic students. Mary Jane Collier, "Communication Competence Problematics in Ethnic Friendships," *Communications Monographs* 63, no. 4 (1996): 314–336.

17. Mary Jane Collier, "A Comparison of Conversations among and between Domestic Culture Groups: How Intra- and Intercultural Competencies Vary," *Communication Quarterly* 36 (1988): 122–124; Mary Jane Collier, "Competent Communication in Intercultural Advisement Contexts," *Howard Journal of Communications* 1 (1988): 3–21.

18. This recalls Dr. Kecia Thomas's work on "pet to threat": Kecia M. Thomas et al., "Women of Color at Midcareer: Going from Pet to Threat," in *The Psychological Health of Women of Color: Intersections, Challenges, and Opportunities,* edited by Lillian Comas-Diaz and Beverly Greene (New York: Guilford Press, 2013), 275–286.

19. Ella Bell Smith and Stella M. Nkomo, *Our Separate Ways: Black and White Women and the Struggle for Professional Identity* (Boston: Harvard Business School Press, 2003).

20. In the United States, *911* is the number to call for emergency assistance as you might need if you were assaulted.

21. Sienna Miller talks about her experience after Boseman's untimely death. Ben Travis, "Chadwick Boseman Boosted Sienna Miller's *21 Bridges* Salary from His Own Pay," *Empire*, September 28, 2020, https://www.empireonline.com/movies/news /chadwick-boseman-boosted-sienna-miller-s-21-bridges-salary-from-his-own-pay/.

22. Jessica Mason Pieklo and Imani Gandy, *Boom! Lawyered: The Hidden Secrets of Jess and Imani,* Rewire News Group, July 18, 2019, https://rewirenewsgroup.com /multimedia/podcast/the-hidden-secrets-of-jess-and-imani/.

23. Among other tweets between the two, this is an excellent example of how they communicate about their relationship: Jessica Mason Pieklo (@Hegemommy), "Twitter. A word," Twitter, July 7, 2021, 11:24 p.m., https://twitter.com/Hegemommy /status/1412975744330911746. See also "Interview with Imani Gandy and Jessica Mason Pieklo from Rewire.News," YouTube, February 25, 2019, https://www.youtube.com /watch?v=2h_cPSufyfk.

24. Beth A. Livingston, KC Wagner, Sarah T. Diaz, and Angela Liu. "The Experience of Being Targets of Street Harassment in NYC," https://righttobe.info/wp -content/uploads/2022/02/fact-sheet-the-experience-of-being-targets-of-street -harassment-in-nyc-fact-sheet.docx.pdf.

25. Cornell University International Survey on Street Harassment (see summary at https://righttobe.org/research/cornell-international-survey-on-street-harassment/).

26. A copy of Audre Lorde's 1981 address ("The Uses of Anger: Women Responding to Racism") was reposted here on August 12, 2012: https://www.blackpast.org/african

-american-history/speeches-african-american-history/1981-audre-lorde-uses-anger
-women-responding-racism/.

27. Dave Smith and W. Brad Johnson, *Good Guys: How Men Can Be Better Allies for Women in the Workplace* (Boston: Harvard Business Review Press, 2020).

28. India R. Johnson and Evava S. Pietri, "An Ally You Say? Endorsing White Women as Allies to Encourage Perceptions of Allyship and Organizational Identity-Safety among Black Women," *Group Processes and Intergroup Relations* (2020): https://journals.sagepub.com/doi/10.1177/1368430220975482.

29. The items on the IRI can be accessed here: https://www.eckerd.edu/psychology/iri/.

30. Ciarra Jones, "The Violence of White (and Non-Black PoC) Apologies," Medium .com, June 9, 2020, https://medium.com/@ciarrajones/the-violence-of-white-and-non -black-poc-apologies-d1321c0ccb8e.

31. Rachel Premack and Marguerite Ward, "How to Apologize If You Accidentally Said Something at Work That's Racist, Sexist, or Offensive," *Business Insider*, September 8, 2020, https://www.businessinsider.com/how-to-apologize-at-work -microaggression-2018-7.

32. Jeanne S. Zechmeister, Sofia Garcia, Catherine Romero, and Shona N. Vas, "Don't Apologize Unless You Mean It: A Laboratory Investigation of Forgiveness and Retaliation," *Journal of Social and Clinical Psychology* 23, no. 4 (2004): 532–564, https://doi .org/10.1521/jscp.23.4.532.40309.

33. Angela Davis, *Women, Race and Class* (New York: Vintage, 1983), 67.

34. Elaine Weiss's book *The Woman's Hour: The Great Fight to Win the Vote* (New York, Penguin, 2019) is referenced in Melissa Block, "Yes, Women Could Vote after the 19th Amendment—But Not All Women. Or Men," *Morning Edition*, NPR, August 26, 2020, https://www.npr.org/2020/08/26/904730251/yes-women-could-vote-after-the -19th-amendment-but-not-all-women-or-men.

Chapter 5

1. Adam Smith, *The Wealth of Nations* [1776], https://www.adamsmith.org/the -wealth-of-nations.

2. Paul Ormerod, *Why Most Things Fail: Evolution, Extinction and Economics* (Hoboken, NJ: Wiley, 2007).

3. Kristen Renwick Monroe, "John Donne's People: Explaining Differences between Rational Actors and Altruists through Cognitive Frameworks," *Journal of Politics* 53, no. 2 (1991): 394–433; Simin Michelle Chen, "Women's March Minnesota on Facebook: Effects of Social Connection on Different Types of Collective Action," *New Media and Society* 22, no. 10 (2020): 1785–1807; Emma A. Bäck, Hanna Bäck, and Holly M. Knapton, "Group Belongingness and Collective Action: Effects of Need to Belong and Rejection Sensitivity on Willingness to Participate in Protest Activities," *Scandinavian Journal of Psychology* 56, no. 5 (2015): 537–544.

4. Gerald Marwell and Pamela Oliver, *The Critical Mass in Collective Action* (Cambridge: Cambridge University Press, 1993).

5. Pieter Gijsbertus Klandermans, *The Social Psychology of Protest* (Cambridge: Cambridge University Press, 1997).

6. John F. Dovidio, Samuel L. Gaertner, and Tamar Saguy, "Commonality and the Complexity of 'We': Social Attitudes and Social Change," *Personality and Social Psychology Review* 13, no. 1 (2009): 3–20.

Notes

7. Stephen Wright and Micah Lubensky, "The Struggle for Social Equality: Collective Action Versus Prejudice Reduction," *Intergroup Misunderstandings: Impact of Divergent Social Realities* (2009): 291.

8. Naomi Ellemers and Manuela Barreto, "Collective Action in Modern Times: How Modern Expressions of Prejudice Prevent Collective Action," *Journal of Social Issues* 65, no. 4 (2009): 749–768; Martijn van Zomeren et al., "Put Your Money Where Your Mouth Is! Explaining Collective Action Tendencies through Group-Based Anger and Group Efficacy," *Journal of Personality and Social Psychology* 87, no. 5 (2004): 649–664, https://doi.org/10.1037/0022-3514.87.5.649.

9. Emma F. Thomas et al., "Testing the Social Identity Model of Collective Action Longitudinally and across Structurally Disadvantaged and Advantaged Groups," *Personality and Social Psychology Bulletin* 46, no. 6 (2020): 823–838.

10. Julia C. Becker et al., "Friend or Ally: Whether Cross-Group Contact Undermines Collective Action Depends on What Advantaged Group Members Say (or Don't Say)," *Personality and Social Psychology Bulletin* 39, no. 4 (2013): 442–455.

11. Tiffany Jana, "The Differences between Allies, Accomplices and Co-Conspirators May Surprise You," *An Injustice!*, February 8, 2021, https://aninjusticemag.com/the-differences-between-allies-accomplices-co-conspirators-may-surprise-you-d3fc7fe29c.

12. See J. E. Sumerau et al., "Constructing Allyship and the Persistence of Inequality," *Social Problems* 68, no. 2 (2021): 358–373, for research on how self-identified allies construct their identities: "As a result, they constructed allyship as an identity they have rather than in relation to advocacy they could be doing in their own lives and with other members of privileged groups."

13. See Helena R. M. Radke et al., "Beyond Allyship: Motivations for Advantaged Group Members to Engage in Action for Disadvantaged Groups," *Personality and Social Psychology Review* 24, no. 4 (2020): 291–315; and Rachael S. Pierotti, Milli Lake, and Chloe Lewis, "Equality on His Terms: Doing and Undoing Gender through Men's Discussion Groups," *Gender and Society* 32, no. 4 (2018): 540–562.

14. "We define White allyship as a continuous, reflexive practice of proactively interrogating Whiteness from an intersectionality framework, leveraging one's position of power and privilege, and courageously interrupting the status quo of predominantly White corporate leadership by engaging in prosocial behaviors that foster growth-in-connection and have both the intention and impact of creating mutuality, solidarity, and support of Afro-Diasporic women's career development and leadership advancement in organizations." Samantha E. Erskine and Diana Bilimoria, "White Allyship of Afro-Diasporic Women in the Workplace: A Transformative Strategy for Organizational Change," *Journal of Leadership and Organizational Studies* 26, no. 3 (2019): 319–338.

15. See this link for an interview with Drs. Bell and Nkomo about their book *Our Separate Ways*, which we have cited throughout our book: https://www.msn.com/en-us/news/us/be-a-co-conspirator-how-white-women-can-move-beyond-allyship-to-actually-support-black-women/vi-AAO45Zc.

16. See Ava DuVernay's Wikipedia page for a detailed list of her productions: https://en.wikipedia.org/wiki/Ava_DuVernay.

17. "DGA 2015-16 Episodic Television Diversity Report," Directors Guild of America, September 12, 2016, https://www.dga.org/News/PressReleases/2016/160912-Episodic-Television-Director-Diversity-Report.aspx.

18. Bethonie Butler, "Why Ava DuVernay Hired Only Female Directors for Her New TV Show 'Queen Sugar,'" *Washington Post*, September 15, 2016, https://www .washingtonpost.com/news/arts-and-entertainment/wp/2016/09/15/why-ava-duvernay -hired-only-female-directors-for-her-new-tv-show-queen-sugar.

19. Macy Freeman and Ashley Nguyen, "The Sisterhood behind Oprah and Ava DuVernay's Hit Show, 'Queen Sugar,'" *The Lily*, August 15, 2018, https://www.thelily .com/the-sisterhood-behind-queen-sugar/.

20. Shapiro notes that they were inspired by the success of *Queen Sugar* to aim toward greater representation of women directors. Ben Travers, "How 'UnREAL' Is Really Helping Female Filmmakers Break into TV," *IndieWire*, July 18, 2016, https:// www.indiewire.com/2016/07/unreal-female-filmmakers-directors-afi-sarah-shapiro -season-2-1201706979/; Liz Shannon Miller, "How to Run a TV Show Where Women Directors Can Thrive, According to the Producers of 'UnREAL,'" *IndieWire*, February 26, 2018, https://www.indiewire.com/2018/02/unreal-producers-interview -sarah-gertrude-shapiro-and-stacy-rukeyser-1201933059/.

21. Susanne Bier, "TV Is Opening the Door to Female Directors—Film Needs to Catch Up," *Guardian*, March 5, 2016, https://www.theguardian.com/commentisfree /2016/mar/05/tv-film-female-directors-susanne-bier-the-night-manager-le-carre.

22. Billy Perrigo, "Timnit Gebru Is Not Waiting for Big Tech to Fix AI," *Time*, January 18, 2022, https://time.com/6132399/timnit-gebru-ai-google/.

23. Simonite, "What Really Happened When Google Ousted Timnit Gebru," Wired.com, June 8, 2021, https://www.wired.com/story/google-timnit-gebru-ai-what -really-happened/.

24. Tom Simonite, "What Really Happened When Google Ousted Timnit Gebru."

25. "Google Fires Margaret Mitchell, Another Top Researcher on Its AI Ethics Team," *Guardian*, February 19, 2021, https://www.theguardian.com/technology/2021 /feb/19/google-fires-margaret-mitchell-ai-ethics-team.

26. Charlie Osborne, "Google Fires Top Ethical AI Expert Margaret Mitchell," ZDNet.com, February 22, 2021, https://www.zdnet.com/article/google-fires-top-ethical -ai-expert-margaret-mitchell/.

27. Margaret Mitchell (@mmitchell_ai), "What @timnitGebru articulates is true," Twitter, January 31, 2022, https://twitter.com/mmitchell_ai/status /1488271700735127553?s=20&t=Y5IAFYY-g06NSGB8FMy28g.

28. Natasha Tiku, "Google Fired Its Star AI Researcher One Year Ago. Now She's Launching Her Own Institute," *Washington Post*, December 2, 2021, https://www .washingtonpost.com/technology/2021/12/02/timnit-gebru-dair/; Emma Roth, "Two Members of Google's Ethical AI Group Leave to Join Timnit Gebru's Nonprofit," *The Verge*, February 2, 2022, https://www.theverge.com/2022/2/2/22915079/google-ethical -ai-group-departure-timnit-gebru.

29. Lisa O'Malley, "WashU Creates Diverse Sociology Department from the Ground Up," *Insight into Diversity*, May 17, 2021, https://www.insightintodiversity.com /washu-creates-diverse-sociology-department-from-the-ground-up/.

30. Jennifer Drysdale, "America Ferrera on How Eva Longoria and Friends Have Become Her 'Saving Grace' as a Mom," *ET Online*, February 20, 2019, https://www .etonline.com/america-ferrera-on-how-eva-longoria-and-friends-have-become-her -saving-grace-as-a-mom-exclusive.

31. Originally they had used the name "She Se Puede" in homage to the activist Dolores Huerta. "America Ferrera and Eva Longoria Bastón alongside Latina Leaders

Notes

Launch She Se Puede, a Digital Lifestyle Community for Latinas," *Cision*, August 31, 2020, https://www.prnewswire.com/news-releases/america-ferrera--eva-longoria -baston-alongside-latina-leaders-launch-she-se-puede-a-digital-lifestyle-community-for -latinas-301120725.html.

32. Joanne Rosa, "How Eva Longoria Is Empowering the Latina Community," ABC News, September 11, 2020, https://abcnews.go.com/Entertainment/eva-longoria -empowering-latina-community/story?id=72954503.

33. "Where It All Started," *Poderistas*, March 29, 2020, https://poderistas.com/about /where-it-all-started/; "America Ferrera, Eva Longoria, Lilliana Vazquez to Join Poderistas Second Annual Latinas Make a Difference Summit," Markets Insider press release, September 1, 2021, https://markets.businessinsider.com/news/stocks/america -ferrera-eva-longoria-lilliana-vazquez-to-join-poderistas-second-annual-latinas-make-a -difference-summit-1030773438.

34. See the video here: https://drive.google.com/file/d/128wwrHbDiTdjIDOic0 -Dkjxy84McS5yS/view?usp=sharing.

35. The Shared Sisterhood page on Facebook: https://www.facebook.com/groups /SharedSisterhood.

36. Timothy P. Munyon et al., "The Implications of Coalition Forms for Work Role Innovation, Resource Reallocation, and Performance," *Research in Personnel and Human Resources Management* (Bingley, UK: Emerald, 2014).

Chapter 6

1. Lee Ross, "From the Fundamental Attribution Error to the Truly Fundamental Attribution Error and Beyond: My Research Journey," *Perspectives on Psychological Science* 13, no. 6 (2018): 750–769.

2. W. Keith Campbell and Constantine Sedikides, "Self-Threat Magnifies the Self-Serving Bias: A Meta-Analytic Integration," *Review of General Psychology* 3, no. 1 (1999): 23–43; Bertram F. Malle, "The Actor-Observer Asymmetry in Attribution: A (Surprising) Meta-Analysis," *Psychological Bulletin* 132, no. 6 (2006): 895–919, https://doi .org/10.1037/0033-2909.132.6.895.

3. Sherry K. Watt, "Difficult Dialogues, Privilege and Social Justice: Uses of the Privileged Identity Exploration (PIE) Model in Student Affairs Practice," *College Student Affairs Journal* 26, no. 2 (2007): 114–126.

4. Ella Bell Smith and Stella M. Nkomo, *Our Separate Ways: Black and White Women and the Struggle for Professional Identity* (Boston: Harvard Business School Press, 2003).

5. Nolan L. Cabrera, "'But I'm Oppressed Too': White Male College Students Framing Racial Emotions as Facts and Recreating Racism," *International Journal of Qualitative Studies in Education* 27, no. 6 (2014): 768–784.

6. William B. Swann Jr., "Self-Verification Theory," *Handbook of Theories of Social Psychology* 2 (2011): 23–42.

7. William B. Swann Jr., "The Trouble with Change: Self-Verification and Allegiance to the Self," *Psychological Science* 8, no. 3 (1997): 177–180.

8. William B. Swann Jr. and Stephen J. Read, "Self-Verification Processes: How We Sustain Our Self-Conceptions," *Journal of Experimental Social Psychology* 17, no. 4 (1981): 351–372.

9. Miguel M. Unzueta and Brian S. Lowery, "Defining Racism Safely: The Role of Self-Image Maintenance on White Americans' Conceptions of Racism," *Journal of*

Experimental Social Psychology 44, no. 6 (2008): 1491–1497; Nolan L. Cabrera, "But I'm Oppressed Too."

10. June Price Tangney, "The Self-Conscious Emotions: Shame, Guilt, Embarrassment and Pride," in *Handbook of Cognition and Emotion*, edited by Tim Dalgleish and Mick J. Power, 541–568 (New York: Wiley, 1999), https://doi.org/10.1002/0470013494.ch26.

11. June Price Tangney and Ronda L. Dearing, *Shame and Guilt* (New York: Guilford Press, 2003).

12. Tamara J. Ferguson, Heidi L. Eyre, and Michael Ashbaker, "Unwanted Identities: A Key Variable in Shame–Anger Links and Gender Differences in Shame," *Sex Roles* 42, no. 3 (2000): 133–157.

13. Dirk Lindebaum, Deanna Geddes, and Peter J. Jordan, eds., *Social Functions of Emotion and Talking about Emotion at Work* (Northampton, MA: Edward Elgar Publishing, 2018).

14. Peter Bregman, "Learning Is Supposed to Feel Uncomfortable," hbr.org, August 21, 2019, https://hbr.org/2019/08/learning-is-supposed-to-feel-uncomfortable.

15. Paula Rothenberg, *White Privilege: Essential Readings on the Other Side of Racism* (New York: Worth Publishers, 2016).

16. A number of Brené Brown's quotes can be found on her website: https://brenebrown.com/.

17. Koritha Mitchell, "Identifying White Mediocrity and Know-Your-Place Aggression: A Form of Self-Care," *African American Review* 51, no. 4 (2018): 253–262.

18. Mitchell, "Identifying White Mediocrity and Know-Your-Place Aggression," 253–262.

19. Smith and Nkomo, *Our Separate Ways.*

20. Sheen S. Levine, Charlotte Reypens, and David Stark, "Racial Attention Deficit," *Science Advances* 7, no. 38 (2021).

21. Lee Shepherd and Chloe Evans, "From Gaze to Outrage: The Role of Group-Based Anger in Mediating the Relationship between Sexual Objectification and Collective Action," *Sex Roles* 82, no. 5 (2020): 277–292.

22. Tangney and Dearing, *Shame and Guilt.*

23. Thomas Gilovich, Victoria Husted Medvec, and Kenneth Savitsky, "The Spotlight Effect in Social Judgment: An Egocentric Bias in Estimates of the Salience of One's Own Actions and Appearance," *Journal of Personality and Social Psychology* 78, no. 2 (2000): 211.

24. Tony Simons, "Behavioral Integrity: The Perceived Alignment between Managers' Words and Deeds as a Research Focus," *Organization Science* 13, no. 1 (2002): 18–35.

25. Tony Simons, Hannes Leroy, Veroniek Collewaert, and Stijn Masschelein, "How Leader Alignment of Words and Deeds Affects Followers: A Meta-Analysis of Behavioral Integrity Research," *Journal of Business Ethics* 132, no. 4 (2015): 831–844.

26. Hugh Son, "Appalled: Here's What Wall Street CEOs Are Saying about George Floyd and Protest Rocking US Cities," CNBC.com, June 1, 2020, https://www.cnbc.com/2020/06/01/wall-street-ceos-speak-out-about-george-floyd-and-protests-rocking-us-cities.html; Gillian Friedman, "Here's What Companies Are Promising to Do to Fight Racism," *New York Times*, August 23, 2020, https://www.nytimes.com/article/companies-racism-george-floyd-protests.html.

27. Pippa Stevens, "Companies Are Making Bold Promises about Greater Diversity, but There's a Long Way to Go," CNBC.com, June 11, 2020, https://www.cnbc.com/2020/06/11/companies-are-making-bold-promises-about-greater-diversity-theres-a-long-way-to-go.html; Edward Segal, "One Year Later: How Companies Have Responded to George Floyd's Murder," *Forbes*, May 25, 2021, https://www.forbes.com/sites/edwardsegal/2021/05/25/one-year-later-how-companies-have-responded-to-george-floyds-murder/?sh=2a1cc0201e68.

28. Mitchell, "Identifying White Mediocrity and Know-Your-Place Aggression," 253–262.

29. Linn Van Dyne, Jill W. Graham, and Richard M. Dienesch, "Organizational Citizenship Behavior: Construct Redefinition, Measurement, and Validation," *Academy of Management Journal* 37, no. 4 (1994): 765–802; James R. Detert and Amy C. Edmondson, "Everyday Failures in Organizational Learning: Explaining the High Threshold for Speaking Up at Work," working paper 06-024, Harvard Business School, Boston, 2005.

30. Ibram X. Kendi, *How to Be an Antiracist* (New York: One World, 2019).

31. Yochi Cohen-Charash and Paul E. Spector, "The Role of Justice in Organizations: A Meta-Analysis," *Organizational Behavior and Human Decision Processes* 86, no. 2 (2001): 278–321.

Chapter 7

1. Kim Tran, "The Diversity and Inclusion Industry Has Lost Its Way," *Harper's Bazaar*, March 23, 2021, https://www.harpersbazaar.com/culture/features/a35915670/the-diversity-and-inclusion-industry-has-lost-its-way/.

2. In 2019, leading scholars on diversity, equity, and inclusion contributed to a special HBR series that delved into the problems with current DEI practices. All five essays are worth reading in full. Laura Morgan Roberts and Anthony Mayo, "Toward a Racially Just Workplace," The Big Idea Series/Advancing Black Leaders, hbr.org, November 14, 2019, https://hbr.org/2019/11/toward-a-racially-just-workplace.

3. Stephanie Creary, Nancy Rothbard, and Jared Scruggs, "Improving Workplace Culture through Evidence-Based Diversity, Equity and Inclusion Practices," Wharton School, University of Pennsylvania, May 2021, https://www.wharton.upenn.edu/wp-content/uploads/2021/05/Applied-Insights-Lab-Report.pdf.

4. Frank Dobbin and Alexandra Kalev, "Why Diversity Programs Fail," *Harvard Business Review*, July–August 2016, https://hbr.org/2016/07/why-diversity-programs-fail.

5. David Thomas and Robin Ely, "Making Differences Matter: A New Paradigm for Managing Diversity," *Harvard Business Review*, September–October 1996, https://hbr.org/1996/09/making-differences-matter-a-new-paradigm-for-managing-diversity. A "discrimination and fairness" approach refers to organizations that focus on fair treatment, often in recruitment processes and complying with legal requirements related to equal opportunity and other federal mandates; Robin J. Ely and David A. Thomas, "Cultural Diversity at Work: The Effects of Diversity Perspectives on Work Group Processes and Outcomes," *Administrative Science Quarterly* 46, no. 2 (2001): 229–273.

6. Laura Morgan Roberts, Anthony J. Mayo, and David A. Thomas, *Race, Work, and Leadership: New Perspectives on the Black Experience* (Boston: Harvard Business Review Press, 2019).

7. Dobbin and Kalev, "Why Diversity Programs Fail"; Roberts and Mayo, "Toward a Racially Just Workplace"; Creary, Rothbard, and Scruggs, "Improving Workplace Culture through Evidence-Based Diversity, Equity and Inclusion Practices."

8. The Combahee River Collective Statement can be read in full here: https://americanstudies.yale.edu/sites/default/files/files/Keyword Coalition_Readings.pdf; Ashley Harris, "Co-Founder of the Combahee River Collective to Speak to UHCL," *The Signal*, March 16, 2020, https://www.uhclthesignal.com/wordpress/2020/03/16/co-founder-of-combahee-river-collective-to-speak-to-uhcl/; "Gender, Race, and Generations: A Roundtable Discussion," Wellesley Centers for Women, Research and Action, Spring/Summer 2017, https://www.wcwonline.org/Research-Action-Report-Spring/Summer-2017/gender-race-and-generations-a-roundtable-discussion.

9. Paula Giddings, "A Noble Endeavor: Ida B. Wells and Suffrage," National Park Service Series on Women's Fight for the Vote, https://www.nps.gov/articles/000/a-noble-endeavor-ida-b-wells-barnett-and-suffrage.htm.

10. The historical record of Oscar Stanton DePriest as a representative is available here: https://history.house.gov/People/Detail/12155; Tiffany K. Wayne, ed., *Women's Suffrage: The Complete Guide to the Nineteenth Amendment* (Santa Barbara, CA: ABC-CLIO, 2020).

11. "African American Members of the US Congress: 1870–2020," Congressional Research Service, December 15, 2020, https://sgp.fas.org/crs/misc/RL30378.pdf.

12. Belle Squire was a product of her time, and some of the language she used in her early writing represents further Dig work she would have yet to do before she could work as a partner alongside Wells-Barnett years later. But unlike many of her White counterparts, Squire centered Black women as being particularly hurt by this move and did not elevate White women's rights above her Black sisters. This early writing is perhaps evidence of why Wells-Barnett and Squire were able to forge a Sisterhood in the years after that. You can find a copy of her writings here: https://hdl.handle.net/2027/uva.x001590932.

13. Bethune was also the president of the National Council of Negro Women.

14. Freeman Pollard, *E. D. Nixon: The Life of a Resourceful Activist* (Montgomery, AL: Junebug Books, 2002). E. D. Nixon was credited for being a key organizer of the Montgomery bus boycott; he was a member of the Brotherhood of the Sleeping Car Porters—the first all-Black labor union; he was described by Dr. Martin Luther King Jr. as one of the most important civil rights voices in the Black community; the Martin Luther King, Jr. Research and Education Institute at Stanford has a brief biography of Nixon on its site: https://kinginstitute.stanford.edu/encyclopedia/nixon-edgar-daniel.

15. Virginia Foster Durr, *Outside the Magic Circle* (Tuscaloosa: University of Alabama Press, 1985).

16. Annabel Gutterman, "The History behind the Supporting Women in 'The Glorias,'" *Time*, September 30, 2020, https://time.com/5894877/glorias-movie-activists/; Sherie M. Randolph, "The Lasting Legacy of Florynce Kennedy, Black Feminist Fighter," *Against the Current*, May–June 2011, https://againstthecurrent.org/atc152/p3272/.

17. Sherie M. Randolph, *Florynce "Flo" Kennedy: The Life of a Black Feminist Radical* (Chapel Hill: University of North Carolina Press, 2018), https://uncpress.org/book/9781469642314/florynce-flo-kennedy/.

Notes

18. Importantly, Kennedy insisted that the White women stay at the *public* conference, but private conversations among Black women were also held. Organizers recognized the importance of conversations both within and between groups.

19. Harmony Goldberg, "Domestic Worker Organizing in the United States: Reports from the Field," *International Labor and Working-Class History* 88 (2015): 150–155.

20. The archived website of the "Domestic Workers United" appears here: http://domesticworkersunited.blogspot.com/.

21. The New York chapter of the National Domestic Workers Alliance: https://www.domesticworkers.org/membership/chapters/we-dream-in-black-new-york-chapter/.

22. "Intro 339," NYC Human Rights, https://www1.nyc.gov/site/cchr/media/intro-339.page.

23. Nathan Weiser, "Domestic Workers Demonstrate in Park Slope," *Red Hook Star-Revue*, October 15, 2021, http://www.star-revue.com/domestic-workers-demonstrate-in-park-slope-by-nathan-weiser/; "'Care Forward' Aims to Raise Standards, Enforce Rights for Domestic Workers in Park Slope," News 12 Brooklyn, September 27, 2021, https://brooklyn.news12.com/care-forward-aims-to-raise-standards-enforce-rights-for-domestic-workers-in-park-slope. See information about the We Rise training approach here: https://www.workersrise.org.

24. Jake Sheridan, "Should You Trust Media Bias Charts?" Poynter, November 2, 2021, https://www.poynter.org/fact-checking/media-literacy/2021/should-you-trust-media-bias-charts/.

25. bell hooks, "Sisterhood: Political Solidarity between Women," *Feminist Review* 23, no. 1 (1986): 125–138.

26. Katy Milkman, *How to Change* (New York: Portfolio, 2021), https://www.katymilkman.com/book.

27. The focus on same-race accountability groups was well received, but it was not unanimously lauded. Several White women complained about being segregated from women of color. Fortunately, most of the women who complained were able to learn that Shared Sisterhood is based on a concentric-circles model where you may engage in Dig among people who are racially similar and then Bridge with people who are of all racioethnic backgrounds. This can help to protect historically marginalized people from potentially burdensome and painful Dig work that is often necessary for people from historically dominant people groups.

28. Rachel D. Arnett and Jim Sidanius, "Sacrificing Status for Social Harmony: Concealing Relatively High Status Identities from One's Peers," *Organizational Behavior and Human Decision Processes* 147 (2018): 108–126.

29. Francesca Gino, Ovul Sezer, and Laura Huang, "To Be or Not to Be Your Authentic Self? Catering to Others' Preferences Hinders Performance," *Organizational Behavior and Human Decision Processes* 158 (2020): 83–100.

30. Kim Scott, "Brutal Honesty and Radical Candor," *Radical Candor* (blog), https://www.radicalcandor.com/radical-candor-not-brutal-honesty/.

31. Charlice Hurst, "The Not Here Syndrome," *Stanford Social Innovation Review*, May 3, 2021, doi: 10.48558/djgd-9p08.

32. Eduardo Bonilla-Silva, *Racism without Racists* (Lanham, MD: Rowman & Littlefield, 2014).

33. As cited in Elizabeth Brown-Guillory, ed., *Wines in the Wilderness* (New York: Greenwood Press, 1990), 100. See May Miller, "Harriet Tubman," in Willis Richardson

and May Miller, *Negro History in Thirteen Plays* (Washington, DC: Associated Publishers, 1935), 265–288.

34. The phrase "Don't agonize, organize" was a 1970s slogan popularized during the women's movement. We have seen both Florynce Kennedy and Tish Sommers credited with the slogan, but it is unclear who coined it initially. (See https://www .barrypopik.com/index.php/new_york_city/entry/dont_agonize_organize.)

Index

Index

Index

Index

Index

Index

Acknowledgments

It is with joy that we release *Shared Sisterhood* to you. We are deeply grateful to all the people who shared their stories and inspired us to write this book; we are grateful too to the members of the Shared Sisterhood Facebook group and to those who join us weekly in our Shared Sisterhood Clubhouse room. Your desire to Dig, Bridge and Collectively Act inspires us.

Our special thanks go to Joan Ball and Rebecca Taylor for their feedback on early drafts of our manuscript. Thanks also to Stacey Batiste, Frances Frei, Dr. Christina Edmondson, and Ekemini Uwan for saying yes. Our eternal gratitude to Drs. Ella Bell and Stella Nkomo for blazing a trail with *Our Separate Ways*. Thank you to Amy Bernstein and the rest of the Harvard Business Review *Women at Work* podcast team for their early support. Thanks also to Gretchen Gavett for her excellent editing of our first HBR articles on this topic and her early and enthusiastic support for us both. We are grateful for Michaela Hava, Karanda Bowman, Sarah Greklek, and the Shared Sisterhood Facebook moderating team.

We are very grateful to Courtney Cashman, our editor at Harvard Business Review Press, who believed in us and in the power of Shared Sisterhood from the beginning. Her skill and patience helped to turn our vision into the book you see before you. We also thank the production staff at the Press, led by Anne Starr, for their expertise and attention. We are also grateful to our literary agent, Alia Hanna Habib, and the team at Gernert, who honored us with their optimistic enthusiasm and support.

From Tina Opie

To my husband and best friend, Fred, thank you for creating space for me to develop and execute this idea. From after-school pickup to sports drop-offs to cooking to walks in the woods, you've supported me as no one else could, always looking out for my best interests. You've heard me talk about this for years, and it's a blessing to celebrate with you as Shared Sisterhood manifests in book form. To our children, Kennedy and Chase, I hope you understand that I am committed to this work because I want both of you to be able to fly without the oppressive forces of racism or sexism or anything else holding you back. I love you and hope that I've made you proud. To my parents, Robert and Clara, who, for as long as I can remember, have encouraged me to love and believe in myself, stand up and challenge injustice, and pursue life with authenticity and passion. You taught me that, at the end of the day, all we have is our name. I want mine to mean something. To my two blood sisters, thank you for always answering when I call. To my girlfriends Erika, Carla, Tiffany, and Nicole, we've been rolling as a group for over two decades. Thank you for praying for me and cheering me on. It's wonderful to have a group of friends who truly relish seeing each other achieve our dreams. To the members of the group where I first heard the term "Shared Sisterhood," thank you for trusting me to develop the idea and encouraging me to run with it. That assignment has led to a critical part of my life's work. To JoAnne Yates, who sponsored me as an MLK Fellow at MIT, thank you for providing essential early feedback for this idea. MIT family, thank you for the financial support, lab space, and meetings where I was able to hone my ideas. To the team at Opie Consulting Group, Violeta and Iris, you have helped me create an infrastructure that enabled me to focus on writing this book and delivering Shared Sisterhood solutions to many clients. Thank you for your thoughtfulness, patience and excellence. To Beth, I couldn't have written this book without you. I had the idea for *Shared Sisterhood* for years, but the working draft remained on the shelf. It was only when you and I started working on it together that the pieces fell into place. Thank you for restoring my trust in the notion that deep, authentic connection can occur across differences—even those differences that seem insurmountable. You are my sister, and I'm so grateful to be on this journey with you.

From Beth Livingston

I am forever grateful to my family—my husband, James Huggins, and my children, Lyrah and Oliver Huggins—for their patience, love, and support as Tina and I wrote this book (during a worldwide pandemic, no less!). Without you, I could not have had the time and space to write. Thank you from the bottom of my heart—I love you! *Shared Sisterhood* is about growth and connection, and I would be remiss not to thank those whose love has helped me to grow and whose connection to me has been a sustaining force. To my parents, Brian and Betty Livingston, whose belief in me is infinite, thank you. To Charlice Hurst, your friendship has been my rock, and your talent in writing has ever been my inspiration. To Rob and Mike Livingston, thank you for giving me someone to look up to. I hope you're proud of your little sister! Thank you to my nieces and nephews for your unconditional love and the joy you have brought me ever since I was eleven years old. My sincerest gratitude also goes to Amy Colbert, Rong Su, and Amy Kristof-Brown for their support and feedback throughout this process. You make me better every day. And to Tina—my Sister—this process began because we shared the desire to change the world for the better, and throughout it, we built a foundation of trust and Sisterhood that will span a lifetime. Thank you for being my friend.

About the Authors

Tina Opie, PhD, is an Associate Professor of Management and an award-winning teacher, researcher, consultant, and speaker. She is the founder of Opie Consulting Group, where she advises large firms in the financial services, entertainment, media, beauty, educational, and health care industries. Her research and commentary have appeared in such outlets as NPR; *O, The Oprah Magazine*; the *Washington Post*; the *Boston Globe*; *Business Insider*; and *Harvard Business Review*, in addition to multiple academic journals. Opie is a regular commentator on Harvard Business Review's *Women at Work* podcast and Greater Boston's NPR affiliate television station, WGBH. She is a renowned leadership and culture expert who specializes in using DEI to help organizations craft cultures based on equitable systemic change. Learn more at www.DrTinaOpie.com.

Beth A. Livingston, PhD, is an Associate Professor in Management and Entrepreneurship at the University of Iowa Tippie College of Business. She is a researcher, teacher, speaker, and consultant who is focused on impacting the world for good, particularly in the areas of gender, equity, and the management of work and family. Her research has been published in top academic journals and has been highlighted in outlets such as the *New York Times*, the *Wall Street Journal*, NPR, and *Harvard Business Review*. Her speaking engagements, executive education, and consulting range from discussions of remote work to those of DEI, and from the gender wage gap to domestic violence, at companies and nonprofits such as John Deere, Yves Saint Laurent Beauty, Allsteel, and *Hollaback!* Beth is the proud mother of Lyrah and Oliver and wife of James Huggins. Learn more at www.BethALivingston.com.